FOOTBALL
For Young Players and Parents

FOOTBALL

For Young Players and Parents

by JOE NAMATH

Created and produced with Bob Oates, Jr.
Illustrations by Todd Treadway
Special photography by Rob Brown

SIMON AND SCHUSTER • NEW YORK

I can't stand it
when I hear
someone tell a
boy, "You can't
do that. You're
not good enough."
Kids can *learn*.
They love to
learn. Let's teach
them the right
techniques and see
what they make of
themselves.

COPYRIGHT © 1986 BY NAMANCO PRODUCTIONS, INC.
ALL RIGHTS RESERVED
INCLUDING THE RIGHT OF REPRODUCTION
IN WHOLE OR IN PART IN ANY FORM
PUBLISHED BY SIMON AND SCHUSTER
A DIVISION OF SIMON & SCHUSTER, INC.
SIMON & SCHUSTER BUILDING
ROCKEFELLER CENTER
1230 AVENUE OF THE AMERICAS
NEW YORK, NEW YORK 10020
SIMON AND SCHUSTER AND COLOPHON ARE REGISTERED TRADEMARKS OF SIMON & SCHUSTER, INC.

MANUFACTURED IN THE UNITED STATES OF AMERICA

10   9   8   7   6   5   4   3   2   1

ISBN: 0-671-52325-2

I would like to dedicate this book
to football's coaches,
to the game's great teachers
of the past and present,
whose dedication and creativity
have developed this challenging sport
and shown us how to enjoy ourselves
and improve ourselves,
both physically and mentally.

Acknowledgments

I'd like to thank two groups of people who have helped make this book possible. First I want to mention all the kids who have come through our football camp the past 15 years. I still remember the first day at that first camp back in 1972. I was nervous. I wasn't really sure I knew how to teach youngsters. But I found out that teaching is a joint venture and that when the students and teacher work together, everybody gains and everybody grows. And over the years we've all grown together. I know for sure that without those kids, I never would have learned much about teaching —how to simplify and try to communicate in a direct and understandable way. So I thank them for that. And I also want to thank John and Bill Dockery especially, and all the other pro athletes I've worked with running that camp, for all the help they have given me.

Second, I'd like to thank the many outstanding pros who are quoted in this book. Every pro player knows the basics of the game, but I'm certainly no expert on the fine points of defensive line play or punting. So I thank the many players who responded graciously to our calls for help, and the others who were quoted originally in the *Craftsmen* series of articles written by my co-author, Bob Oates, for *Pro!* magazine.

Among the others who have been a big help to this project: Todd Treadway, of Hellman Design Associates, for his outstanding drawings; Dave Boss, Creative Director of NFL Properties, for his excellent choice in photographs; George Allen, a championship coach and great student of the game, for his help on football drills; Bob Engle, 25 years the cover editor of *Newsweek* magazine, for his masterful management of a last-minute photographic assignment; Rob Brown, the highly-regarded West Coast photographer, for his professional and amazingly efficient photography of young players working with me; Duke Dulgarian, head coach of the St. Bernard Vikings (Playa del Rey, California), plus the many Vikings players, for their energetic modeling in those photographs; Pearl Smith and Rich Reever, head coach and defensive coordinator of the Fairfield (Iowa) High School Trojans, for their insights into modern high school football; Jim Wickboldt, for his exercise expertise and informed reading of the manuscript; and Louise Payne and Phil Barber of NFL Properties, for their nearly instantaneous work in the huge NFL Properties photo file. Finally, at Simon & Schuster we have many people to thank. First comes Editor-In-Chief Michael Korda, for conceiving this project originally and suggesting it to us; then Don Hutter, Herman Gollob and Bob Bender, for their astute and good-humored editorial input; and finally, Jeanne Palmer, production manager, for a caring and careful job creating the finished product.

Contents

PREFACE: TO PARENTS AND FANS　　　　　**12**

INTRODUCTION: WHAT IT TAKES　　　　　**16**

Teamwork 18　　　　　　　　Using Your Head 24
Courage & Self-Discipline 20　Handling Mistakes 28
Desire and Technique 22

PART ONE: THE BASICS　　　　　　　　　**32**

The Basics 34　　　　　　　Agility 52
The Field 36　　　　　　　Speed 54
The Game 38　　　　　　　The Hitting Position 58
Choosing a Position 40　　　Stance and Start 60
Equipment 44　　　　　　　Leverage 64
Strength 46　　　　　　　Basic Shoulder Block 66
Flexibility 48　　　　　　　Tackling 72
Endurance 50

PART TWO: THE RUNNING GAME　　　　　**78**

The Running Game 80　　　　*•Picking The Hole 98*
The Quarterback 82　　　　　*•Faking Them Tight 100*
　•The Snap 84　　　　　　*•The Stiff-Arm 102*
　•The Pivot 86　　　　　The Blockers 104
　•The Handoff 88　　　　　*•Pulling Out 106*
　•The Pitchout 90　　　　　*•The Trap Block 110*
The Runner 92　　　　　　　*•The Cross-Block 112*
　•The Runner's Lean 94　　　*•Downfield Blocking 114*
　•Follow Your Blockers 96　*•Backs As Blockers 116*

PART THREE: STOPPING THE RUN　　　　　**118**

Stopping The Run 120　　　　*•Containment 138*
The Line 122　　　　　　　*•The Shuffle 140*
　•Attack Your Man 124　　　*•Chasing The Runner 142*
　•Shedding Your Man 126　The Secondary 144
　•Shooting The Gap 128　　*•Run Support 146*
　•Reading Your Man 130　　*•Hanging On 148*
The Linebackers 132　　　　Gang Tackling 150
　•Reading The Play 134　　Pursuit Angles 152
　•Playing Off Blockers 136　Stripping The Ball 154

PART FOUR: THE PASSING GAME 156

The Passing Game 158
The Quarterback 160
•The Grip 166
•Turning To Throw 168
•The Dropback 170
•The Set Up 176
•Footwork 178
•Throwing On The Run 180
The Receivers 182
•The Release 184
•Driving Them Off 186
•Pass Routes 188
•Beating The Zone 190
•Concentration 192
•Catching The Ball 194
•Tight Ends And Backs 198
The Line 200
•Retreating 202
•The Hit 204
•The Recoil 206

PART FIVE: STOPPING THE PASS 208

Stopping The Pass 210
The Rush Line 212
•The Rip Move 214
•The Swim Technique 216
•Hands High 218
The Linebackers 220
•The Drop 222
•Playing Man-To-Man 224
•The Blitz 226
The Secondary 228
•The Backpedal 230
•Man-To-Man 232
•Playing Zone 234
•Driving On The Ball 236

PART SIX: THE KICKING GAME 238

The Kicking Game 240
The Punt 242
The Place Kick 244
The Kicker's Mind 252
The Invisible Heroes 254
Kick Coverage 256
Kick Returns 258

GLOSSARY 260

To Parents And Fans

This is a book about football. I designed it originally with the young player in mind—but I think any football fan can enjoy it. How do the great players do what they do? What are the basic techniques that make for winners and champions? These are the questions we've tried to answer—and any place we weren't sure, we've gone out and collected quotes from the game's best players. The young player should be able to read this book and learn, step-by-step, how to play the game. And fans should find here the inside story behind the dramatic action they see every week.

I'll tell you a group I've thought about a lot while working on this book. The family. I'd love to think that parents and kids could read this book, learn some things, maybe talk about and work on some of the things together. Even moms, maybe they can find out why their children like football so much, why they want to play, what it is they accomplish.

It's in my mind because my own family was so supportive of me when I was young. My mother and father were really behind me, and from my older brothers I learned some important basics—some of the types of things we are showing in this book. It all really gave me an advantage, and I'd like to pass on that kind of advantage to young players today.

Kids can learn. They love to learn. They love to get better at things. We see this every summer at our football camp for boys. We've been running this camp every year for 15 years. I've hardly missed a day—and one reason is how much I enjoy being with young players while they learn and grow. If we teach boys the right techniques, the basics, at an early age, they improve. They do well. They succeed. And then they can enjoy one of the great experiences I know about: working and winning as part of a football team.

I can't stand it when I hear someone tell a boy, "You can't do that. You're not good enough." You've heard people say things like that. "You can't play quarterback. You'll have to play defense." My nephew Franklin is a good lineman, playing in high school. Last fall some coach comes down from a college and tells him, "You're not quick enough to play guard. You'd better concentrate on tackle." Please! *We're* young. *We* can grow. Teach us the right techniques, and let's see what we can do. Don't tell us we can't do something.

There's a line in Richard Bach's book, *Illusions*, that has really stuck with me: "Argue for your limitations—and they're yours." I'm convinced that's true. And that's why we don't want kids thinking negative. We don't want them thinking about their limitations. We don't want them thinking, "Can't."

It really does bother me. Coaches put limitations on kids, teachers put limitations on kids, sometimes even parents put limitations on kids. They do it out of love. The teachers, the parents—they love the children, and they don't want to see them disappointed. So they try to tell them early, "You can't do this." Try to get them to aim low so they won't be disappointed. But I think it's a terrible mistake. Who knows what the child can do? He's still growing. He's still learning. You teach that child the right techniques, give him the right direction—in football or anything else—and he can change himself completely. Even physically, a kid can change his whole physical being, make himself stronger, faster, quicker, tougher. I see kids do it all the time.

I'll tell you a football player who proved this point. I'm talking about George Sauer, who played wide receiver with me on the New York Jets. Now George would be the first to tell you he was no brilliant athlete. He wasn't fast. He wasn't very big. He wasn't really graceful. But George Sauer made himself into an All-Pro. He loved to practice. He always asked me to stay out after practice and throw to him. He would work on new patterns, first walking them off step-by-step, then trotting, then going all-out. He'd have

Our role is to teach them the right techniques —and encourage them to do whatever they want (as long as it's not something harmful). Teach them and encourage them.

You can make yourself better—that's one point to this book. Any young athlete can grow and improve. We just teach them and encourage them.

every move down to that last split-second, and he worked so hard on it you could always count on him in a game. He was technically on the money. He was mentally on the money. And in our Super Bowl game, he caught eight passes, a record at that time.

You can *make* yourself better—and that's one point to this book. Any young athlete can grow and improve. So let's get together and see how far each child can go. It seems to me that as adults and parents, our role is to teach them the basics—and encourage them to do whatever they want (as long as it's not harmful). Teach them and encourage them. And let's see what they make of themselves.

I know that's the kind of support I got when I was young, back home in Beaver Falls, Pennsylvania. My mother, it's true, didn't go see me play very much. She was afraid I'd get hurt. Even when I was playing in college and the pros, she'd sit in front of her television with her rosary in her hand and the candles lit, praying I wouldn't get hurt. It worked, too, some of the time. But she was always behind me, and she liked sports. In fact, if you got her going, she'd tell you what a big basketball star she was when she was younger.

My dad really loved sports, too. He'd take off on a weekend and drive to Chicago to see a big boxing match. He hadn't had the chance to play much when he was a kid. He came over from Hungary when he was 13, and it was time to go to work about the time he arrived in America. He spent 40 years in the steel mills. But he became a big sports fan, and he was sometimes the business manager for our Little League football teams and our Knee-High baseball teams.

As far as technical training goes, my big brothers gave me a tremendous amount of help. They all worked with me, and brother Bob really did give me excellent advice about how to throw a football. He was nine years older and he had been a quarterback, and it was Bob who first showed me the proper throwing motion. We'd play catch out in the street, and he would *not* allow me to use a big wind-up. "Right from the ear, right from the ear," he'd say. "Winding up is for a baseball pitcher."

I was lucky. Right from the beginning I was shown the right techniques, so I was a pretty good passer even when I was ten or eleven years old. We'd have good games right out there in the street, all my family including my older sister Rita, who was a terrific athlete, plus the neighborhood kids, and they'd let the little kid play because I could throw well enough. Then sometimes we'd organize a team from the Lower End, and we'd go up to the projects and play those guys. They had a field up there and we'd play tackle, no pads—which is crazy, and I'd never recommend it to anybody; if a youngster wants to play tackle today, he should join a Pee Wee league. But it's all we had. I'd play quarterback on offense, or sometimes halfback or receiver. Then on defense I'd play nose tackle. That's right. In the middle of the line. The kids from the projects played a split-T offense, and, if you were quick, you could jump right over the center and get the quarterback before he started his play.

Anyway, it all helped, especially the family support and learning good techniques. And that's one reason I've done this book. I'd like to see kids today have the same advantage I had —especially learning the right techniques at an early age. Maybe you'll want to read the book and then work right along with your children, helping coach them and get them ready. Or maybe you'll just want to know what's in here so you can talk with your kids and know what it is they're doing. Some children really want help from their folks. Others just want to know their parents care about what they're up to.

Whichever suits your family, I hope we can work together and help your children learn the game and enjoy themselves.

It was my brother Bob who first showed me the proper throwing motion. I was lucky. Right from the beginning I was shown the right techniques.

15

INTRODUCTION

What It Takes

Teamwork

Football is a wonderful game. I love it. I'll tell you one reason why: it's an honest game. It's true to life. It's a game about sharing.

I believe that most of life is sharing and working together. There isn't too much you can do in life all by yourself. For instance, I'm sometimes on TV. Well, *I* don't do TV. *We* do TV. We've got directors and camera people and production people—a whole *team* that let's me stand up there and be on TV. Or maybe you want to get in your car and drive downtown. Well, somebody else made the car, somebody else keeps it running, somebody else keeps up the roads. It's the truth, man. You don't do very much on your own.

Playing football, you learn this better than any way I know. In football, the best quarterback or the best halfback in the world isn't going to get much done if his buddies up front don't block people. Football is a team game, and that's why I love it. In fact, I like that part of it so much that even when I wanted to name my fishing boat, I called it *Team Game*.

The thing is, a team game is just so much fun. You're working together. You're sharing an adventure. You've got your buddies there with you when times are good—and also when times are bad. When things get tough, it's awful to be alone. A time like that, you're lucky to have your teammates to reach out to. When times are good, when you've won a big game and you're feeling great, it's much more fun to celebrate and share the accomplishment with your friends.

So football is a team game, and life is a team game. That's one reason I like to help boys learn to play this sport. We can learn what *life* is about by learning the game. As soon as the boys start arriving at our summer football camp, we start to eliminate that "I" word and start putting in the "We" word. *We* can do this. *We* can do that. Each boy has to work hard himself, master the basic techniques, get good at his own position. But it's by working together that a team can move down the field and score some points. You do get great individual efforts from time to time, sure. But it's by working together that you get to know the real fun of the sport.

I'll tell you another thing that teamwork means in football. It means listen to your coach. I see some youngsters come to play football who aren't used to being bossed around. Maybe at home they get to do nearly anything they want. They might be a little pampered. When those kids first run into a football coach, they may be a bit shocked.

But football isn't a democracy. The game is so complicated that somebody has to be in charge. That somebody is the coach. The thing for you to do is adjust to the situation and learn what you can from it. You may not agree with every-thing the coach is doing, and sometimes you may be right. Coaches make mistakes like everybody else. But if you waste your time being mad at your coach, you won't be able to learn from him. You won't be able to help your team. If you think your coach is really a bad man, ask your parents to come see him work. But otherwise, let the coach be the coach. You be a player. That's the way a football team works.

The thing is, a team game is just so much fun. You're working together. You're really sharing an adventure.

Sharing the big plays and the big wins with your teammates makes the whole game a lot more fun.

PHOTO: BILL WEDDLE

Courage and Self-Discipline

You learn you can do your best even when it's hard, even when you're tired and maybe hurting a little bit. It feels good to show some courage.

Football is a hard-knocking sport. This isn't ping pong or checkers we're talking about. It's a tough game, and if you want to play, you have to show some courage.

But I'll tell you something else. Once you learn some of the skills of blocking and tackling, once you've hit some big guy and lived to tell about it, it doesn't seem so bad anymore. The rules of the game protect you. You wear good equipment. You learn how to handle yourself. Pretty soon you're a football player and holding up your end for your teammates.

You learn something about yourself in the process. You learn you can do your best even when it's hard, even when you're tired and maybe hurting a little bit. You're going to get your share of bumps and bruises. You're going to get your foot stepped on or your knuckles cut up. Then you'll find out you can still play hard, still do your job.

I don't mean you act stupid. If you really get hurt—if you strain a muscle or sprain an ankle—you come right out of the game and let a doctor look at you. But the little bumps and bruises, it's a good feeling when they don't stop you. A man feels good when he shows some courage, some toughness.

Two things can help you handle the combat. First, choose a position that makes sense for you. If you're a little guy, you don't belong in the middle of the line. A little guy should show his courage as a wide receiver, maybe, or a safety.

Second, you need some self-discipline. The only way to do well during a game is to work hard during practice. Learn the right techniques. Practice until you have them perfect. Come early to practice, get as much out of every minute as you can, then stay out afterward and do a little extra.

I've got a piece of paper in my wallet with a sentence I wrote on it years ago. It says, "I believe a necessary quality of one's good character is discipline." I do. And if you show some discipline—if you learn how to block and tackle right—it also gives you courage. Discipline and courage go together.

It feels great to win a tough game, to show courage and self-discipline and come out on top.

Desire and Technique

If you *want* to play football, you *can* play football. If you want to make yourself into a football player, you can do it.

ere's something really good about football. There are 22 positions on every team—plus kickers and special teams players and important substitutes. There is *room* on a football team. There's room for little guys, room for big heavy guys, room for guys who aren't great athletes.

Here is my point. If you *want* to play football, you *can* play football—for sure up through high school, and often right into the pros. I think of George Sauer again. Or look at Joe Morris—he's only 5 feet 7 inches tall, but he's a Pro Bowl runner with the New York Giants. And what about Lionel (Train) James? He's another little guy, only 5-6, and he came to the San Diego Chargers with not much reputation. But he set an all-time NFL mark gaining 2535 all-purpose yards in 1985 ("all-purpose yards" means running from scrimmage, running kicks and catching passes).

If these guys can do it, you can do it. Football is a tough game, but it's a game you can get into on sheer desire. If you want to make yourself into a football player, you can do it, and you can play on a team and have all the fun of working together with your buddies. As the coaches always say, "You've got to *want* it."

But there is one more thing you need besides desire. You need technique. You've got to know what you're doing out there. You can have all the desire in the world—you can be ready to run right over a guy and make yourself a hero—but if that guy knows the proper techniques and you don't, he's going to make you look pretty foolish. He's going to hit you under your pads and stand you up where your feet can't drive. Then he's just going to toss you. Just brush you off.

The thing is, in football a smaller guy can win the battle—if he knows the right techniques. A guy with less ability can win the battle—if he knows what he's doing.

You've got to know techniques. Not just the techniques of blocking and tackling. Not just the techniques of throwing

Lionel (Train) James looks small, but he runs big because he has desire. He holds the NFL record for all-purpose yards in one season, 2535 in 1985.

JIM CHAFFIN

and catching and kicking. You've got to know mental techniques—how to use your head. You've got to know training techniques—how to make yourself stronger, faster, more agile. Playing football, you get to become better in many ways. You get to become a disciplined person who knows how to improve himself.

This is a great thing because as we go through life, we're *supposed* to get better. We're supposed to *improve*. Even a puppy is expected to learn some things, to learn how to behave, to improve himself. Living means improving.

Maybe right now we aren't playing as well as we want. That's all right. We're going to grow. We're going to get bigger and stronger. We're going to learn how to play better.

23

Using Your Head

You're football smart if you understand the game. If you understand your position. If you know all the basic techniques and when to use each one.

You have to use your head to play football. The smarter team always has a big advantage in any football game. The smarter player has an edge in any match-up. I'm not talking about IQ here. I don't mean math smart or English smart, although those are great. I'm talking about football smart. You're football smart if you understand the game. If you understand your position. If you know all the basic techniques and when to use each one.

Smart teams usually win. When I was a freshman at the University of Alabama, I learned a good football lesson from Coach Paul Bryant. In one of the first meetings he said, "To win, we first must not beat ourselves." I've learned how true that is. Winning often comes down to the team that doesn't make mistakes and bust assignments and throw the ball to the wrong team. To the team that plays a smart game.

I know our Super Bowl team with the New York Jets was a smart one [the 1968 team that won Super Bowl III]. I don't just mean Joe Namath, the quarterback. I mean the whole team. I think we showed it when we beat the Baltimore Colts in that Super Bowl. The Colts played a very confusing defense. Sometimes they laid back in a deep zone pass defense. Sometimes they blitzed nearly everybody, eight guys, a "maximum blitz." How do you beat a defense like that? You've got to play it smart.

First, all your blockers have to be smart enough to figure out the blitz, to see who's coming where, and get everybody blocked. And we had guys who could think that fast, guys like Winston Hill and Dave Herman in the line and guys like Emerson Boozer and Matt Snell in the backfield. These guys could think on their feet. They knew their assignments. They adjusted fast. I didn't have any blitzers in my face right away.

Then our receivers had to be smart enough to change their patterns. With an all-out blitz coming, a quarterback can't stand around and wait for some deep pass pattern to develop.

Quarterbacks have to
be alert all the time,
telling their team-
mates what to do and
who to watch out for.
But all good football
players have to use
their heads, every
play of every game.

> Usually a young player will hear the play in the huddle, and then his mind will begin to wander. You need a mental checklist to go over after you hear the play.

What we did was to use "automatic" passes. Our wide receivers had to look inside and watch the safetymen. If the safety blitzed, the wide receiver had to change whatever pattern he was running and just break it off quickly on a short slant pattern to the inside. With a receiver like George Sauer, that could work. He had to think fast, and he did. He had prepared himself mentally, working on it over and over in practice. He had his head in the game. And whenever that safety blitzed, Bam! we completed a pass right where he used to be.

Later in the game, we changed things even more. The point is, we won that game because we were mentally ready. We used our heads.

How do you do this? What is a good mental technique for youngsters to use? I'll tell you what I recommend to all the young players I coach at our summer camp. I tell every player to use a *mental checklist* before every play.

What I mean is this: usually a young running back, say, will get in the huddle, hear the play called, and then his mind will begin to wander aimlessly. He comes out of the huddle, and he's not thinking about anything in particular. Then he looks over at the defense and he sees some big linebacker and he starts thinking, "Oh, my gosh, what if that big guy gets a shot at *me*." Right then the ball is snapped and the running back hasn't any idea what to do. If he's lucky, he'll just stand there. But probably he'll run into the quarterback and cause a fumble or do something stupid. Because he's not *using* his mind. He's just letting his mind roam around free. He's being mentally lazy.

So what I recommend is this: every player should have a mental checklist that he goes over before each play. For instance, that running back hears the play in the huddle. Now his checklist could go like this. As he comes out of the huddle, first he repeats the snap count in his mind. Then he remembers where his blockers are going to open a hole for him. Then—and this is very important—he visualizes where he needs to run so the quarterback can hand him the ball—what we call the *exchange point*. Finally, he thinks of the snap count again.

It's a checklist. One, two, three, four. Count, hole, exchange point, count. After you do it a few times, it becomes a habit. And what happens when the ball is snapped? You run the play. You run it right. It's automatic. You haven't got room in your mind to worry about the other guys because you're *using* your mind to help you play.

At other positions, you would have a different checklist. An offensive guard might go: Snap count. Imagine blocking the right man. Imagine blocking him the right way. Snap count. A wide receiver might go: Snap count. Imagine running your pattern. Imagine catching the ball. Snap count.

The point is, *use* your mind—and don't waste time. That time between the huddle and the play isn't just dead time. That's as important as the play itself. That's when you plan to make yourself successful.

The same thing is true on the sideline. That's not vacation time. You rest up your body, but your mind is still in the game. If you play defensive back, maybe you watch the defensive backs on the other team. Try to learn something from them. Or try to realize when they are making a mistake.

Keep watching. Keep thinking. Keep learning. Every practice is so important. Every game is such a great experience. We should try to grow every minute. We should get better all the time—whether we're talking about football, or schoolwork or anything else we do.

You can learn how to do this. You can learn to *use* your mind. It's just like training the body. You keep using the mind and pretty soon it gets greased. It gets oiled. It operates more smoothly. This will help you in football, and it will give you mental discipline that will help you all your life.

You can learn to *use* your mind. It's just like training the body. It will help you in football. And it will give you mental discipline that will help you in life.

Handling Mistakes

I believe this is the best way to handle a mistake: *learn* from it. Don't worry about it. Don't agonize over it. Just learn from it so you become a better football player—and a better person.

Here's the last thing I want to talk about in this introduction. I want to tell you how to handle mistakes. Because—believe me—you're going to make mistakes while you learn how to play the game of football.

You may wonder how I know that's true. Well, I have to admit I've made a few mistakes in my time. I'll own up to it. In fact, I think I hold an all-time record that fortunately isn't talked about much. Know what it is? One day I threw six interceptions—in one *half*. Six interceptions in thirty minutes of football. What is that—one every five minutes? I couldn't believe it.

Now I don't mean I threw six terrible passes. We had a couple of tipped balls in there, and the last one was a desperation pass on the final play of the game. But still—I'm trying to keep up my confidence, and here come six guys in Houston Oiler uniforms running my passes back at me.

How do you handle mistakes like that? There are things to do, and I tried to do them. I kept telling myself to relax, so I wouldn't press and force a bad play. I went back to the plays I felt most comfortable with, the things I could do best. Those are good tips. They usually work. But not this day. *Nothing* worked on this day. Six interceptions.

Let me tell you how it ended. In the last few minutes, Don Maynard caught a two-point conversion pass, and at least we tied up the score. Now it was 28-28, and we got the ball back one last time. On the last play of the game I threw that desperation bomb from about my own 35. Naturally it bounced around and got intercepted. So all right. Game's over. As their guy is getting tackled, I'm walking off the field—and then that guy *laterals* the ball. OK, I jump back into a football position, get ready to help. But then this second guy is being tackled. I start off the field again—and *he* laterals. I think they lateraled four times on that one play. It ends up with Kenny Houston, an All-Pro safety, running down the

Lester Hayes (37) and Mike Haynes of the Raiders discuss their assignments. If you make a mistake, talk it over with another player. Or go ask your coach. Find out what you did wrong so you can correct it. And when a coach is explaining things to another player, *listen*. There is plenty you can learn

sideline with the ball, and he's got his middle linebacker, Garland Boyette, in front of him. And you know who's back to stop them? Yep. Me. And Don Maynard, who's 170 pounds in his full uniform. How'd you like to be a coach and your whole game comes down to Joe Namath and Don Maynard playing defense for you?

So here comes that big Boyette in front, and the only advantage I had was, Boyette was *tired*. This is the last play of the game, and he's just run all over the field on this one play, and he is really puffing. I get my hands on him like a linebacker is supposed to and somehow I manage to play him right into the ground as he tries to block me. Meanwhile Houston is almost past. I jump at him and all I get is a foot and just then

When you make a mistake it isn't going to feel good; it's not *supposed* to feel good. But don't let yourself be upset about it for too long.

Maynard comes across and hits him. Between us we just do get him out of bounds. On the *four* yard-line.

I tell you what, if I had thrown six interceptions *plus* they ran the last one right past me for the touchdown to beat us, I *really* would have felt bad. I don't mean I felt exactly good, but at least we got out of it with a tie.

So I know about mistakes. Any football player knows about mistakes. All you have to understand about mistakes is this: we *all* make them. It's human to err. When you make a mistake it isn't going to feel good; it's not *supposed* to feel good. But don't let yourself be upset about it for too long. You should develop some discipline. Don't just wallow in the sorrow of that mistake and waste a lot of time feeling sorry for yourself. Instead, do something useful. And what's useful is to find out what happened, recognize the cause of your mistake, and do what you need to correct it.

Let's say you're playing offensive tackle and you block the wrong guy. The guy you were *supposed* to block goes through and flattens your quarterback. Now what do you do? Well, what you *don't* do is get all upset. Too many young players let a mistake get to them. They won't talk about it. They throw their helmet and go sit on the bench and sulk. To put it in a nutshell: they waste a lot of time. They don't help themselves, and they don't help their team.

Find the cause of your mistake and correct it. If you don't know your plays, for instance, *learn* your plays. If you took your eyes off a pass and dropped it, practice catching hundreds of passes and watch every last one into your hands. In other words, learn from your mistakes. If you get better every time you make a mistake, you'll become a fine football player.

One more thing about mistakes. Don't be the kind of player that hollers at his teammates for mistakes. Or sneaks around behind their backs and badmouths them for mistakes. A lot of young players have this tendency to point the finger at their teammates, and it's really a weak attitude. In the first place, we all make mistakes, including *you*. In the second place, not every "mistake" is really anyone's fault. Maybe on a dropped pass the sun was a problem. Or maybe the defense just made a good play. Then hats off to *them*. That's not a mistake.

But whatever happened, don't go hollering at your teammates. That just makes them feel worse and slows down their learning. And if they don't improve, then your *team* gets hurt. You win and lose with your teammates. So pick them up.

I can give you an example of this, too. We were playing Miami, and I really needed a pick-up. It was the only game I ever played where I didn't really have my head into it. The thing was, my dad was in the hospital. He got better again after that, thank God, but during the game I guess it really affected me. I wasn't playing all that well, and we were behind late in the game. I was feeling like I was letting my teammates down. It was a really bad feeling, and I was just sitting there on the bench with my head down.

Then our halfback, Emerson Boozer, came over and sat down with me. He put his arm on my shoulder and said, "Hey, don't be down, man. Don't worry. We'll get the ball back and score. We're going to win this game." I'll tell you what. I really appreciated that. Usually, I felt it was *my* job to pick guys up, but here when I was down my teammate came over to help me out. It really made a difference to me. And you know what? A few plays later Miami fumbled, and we *did* go in and score, and we did win that game.

So don't criticize your teammates. It's one of the most important things I've learned: treat other people like *you* want to be treated. Or like you want your mother and father treated, or any of your friends. Be kind to them. Encourage them. Pick them up. Your teammates will like you better, your team will *get* better, and you'll enjoy yourself a whole lot more.

You're in it with your teammates. Pick them up. Encourage them when they make mistakes. Make them feel better and they'll learn more quickly.

PART ONE

The
Basics

The Basics

If you want to be a winner, you must start with the basics of the game. Not everyone understands that. Sometimes we find a youngster who just wants to be a hero—who wants to go out and catch touchdown passes or make big tackles without getting ready first. He wants to *be* a hero, but he doesn't know how to *make* himself a hero.

It's very simple. To do your best, you have to master the basics. If you want to build the Empire State building, or the Great Pyramid, first you have to lay down a solid foundation. You can't build on mud or sand. You need to get a firm basis, and then you can build way up high.

It's just like that in football. If you master the basics of the game, then you can make the big plays. If you have a good stance and a good start, if you can work comfortably in the basic hitting position, if you know how to get leverage on your opponent—in other words, if you know the basics of the game—then you can play football at most any position. You can hold up your end and do a good job for yourself and for your teammates. A guy who has mastered the basics, who has made himself into a solid, all-around football player—that's the guy who will get the most out of the game.

At our football camp, we sometimes see an older boy who doesn't want to go back and work on basics. He figures he has been playing two or three years and had some success —so why should he work on the simple things? But that boy doesn't know how much better he could be. He doesn't realize that he's not consistent, that he makes one good play on natural talent and then one bad one because he doesn't know what he's doing. He wonders why some younger kid can beat him off the line, or why some smaller guy can block him and push him around. He should work on the basics.

What *are* the basics? First, you should have a good understanding of the game. You should know the field, the basic rules, the equipment, and the various positions. Then you should build yourself up as an athlete. Spend some time working on your strength and speed, on your flexibility and agility and endurance. Finally, you need to work on the basic football techniques. You need a well-balanced stance and an explosive start. You need to get comfortable in the basic hitting position and learn how to get under your opponent and use leverage to control him. And you need to master the basic techniques of blocking and tackling.

We cover all that in this section. The information is here. Now what it takes from you is *commitment*. Commitment and *dedication*. If you want to buy a pizza, you have to put your money on the line—you have to commit your cash. If you want to be a football player, you have to commit *yourself*. You have to dedicate your time, your body, and your mind.

The fact is, it's fun to dedicate yourself, to put in the time to make yourself better. It's fun and exciting and challenging. And you have to do it. Without commitment and dedication, the best athlete in the world isn't going very far.

I'll tell you what I mean. I would *never* throw a pass with poor technique. Even warming up, I never set my feet casually, or used my body incorrectly. Even on the sidelines, I set up just like I would in the pocket in a game. I did that because good coaches convinced me that if you practice the basics right all the time, you'll do them right in the game.

Here's what this all comes down to: human beings are creatures of habit. We do things the way we are *used* to doing them. So why not create *good* habits? We're going to play football and other sports anyway. Why not use our time to create good habits and get the most from our God-given talents? It's not hard to develop good habits—in sports, in class, on the job, or wherever. It only takes a little commitment, a little dedication. Just listen to the people who know, do what they say, and master the basics. You'll make yourself a winner. And you'll be glad you deveoped good habits.

The Field

If you want to play football, you ought to know the field well. If you haven't played much football, go play some catch on one with your friends, so you get totally comfortable with the dimensions.

How long is a football field? One hundred yards? Not really. It's true a football field is one hundred yards from goal line to goal line—but then there are two ten-yard end zones. A football *field* is 120 yards long.

How wide is it? Do you know? I'll bet there are a lot of pros who don't know. It's 53 yards—plus one foot. Fifty-three and one-third yards.

These may sound like small things, but if you want to play football, you ought to know the field well. If you haven't played much football, go play some catch on one with your friends, so you get totally comfortable with the dimensions.

Sideline: A line up and down each side for all 120 yards. If any part of the runner or the ball touches on or outside the sideline, he is out of bounds.

Goal Line: The line you need to cross to score a touchdown. The offensive team tries to advance down the field to cross the goal line protected by the defensive team.

End Zone: The ten yards from the goal line to the end line.

End Line: The back of the end zone; plays like a sideline.

Hashmarks: Small lines parallel with the sidelines. Their distance from the sideline is different at each level of football. If an offensive play ends up outside the hash-marks, the ball is brought in even with the hashmarks to start the next play.

Goal Posts: Posts set in the middle of each end line, shaped like tuning forks. Field goal kicks and extra points must go over the crossbar and "through" the uprights (actually, they can go high over the crossbar within an imaginary, straight-up extension of the two uprights).

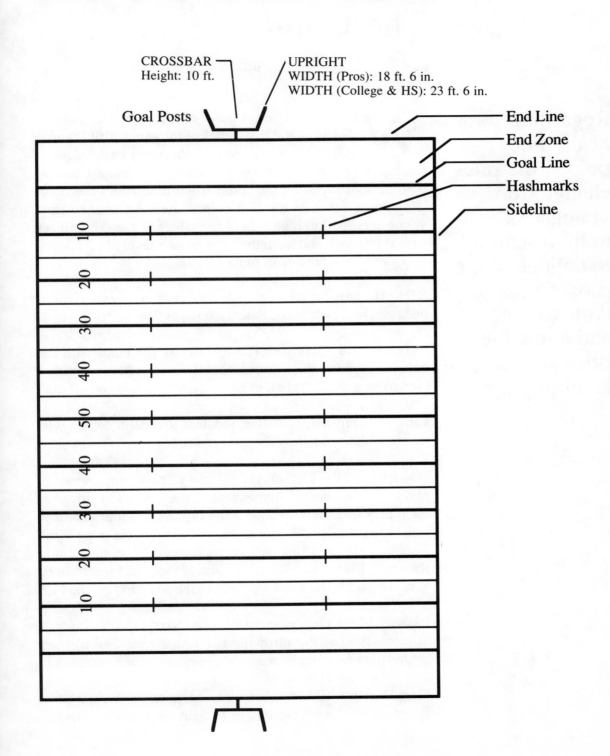

CROSSBAR
Height: 10 ft.

UPRIGHT
WIDTH (Pros): 18 ft. 6 in.
WIDTH (College & HS): 23 ft. 6 in.

Goal Posts

End Line
End Zone
Goal Line
Hashmarks
Sideline

10
20
30
40
50
40
30
20
10

The Game

Regarding some of the fine points, the rules change from youngsters' ball to high school to college to the pros. Check with your coach and know the rules at your level of play.

Writing this book, I assume you know the game of football—the basic rules of the game. Still I think it will help to list some of the most basic ideas of football right here. Plus, in the back you'll find a Glossary with definitions of all the football words I use in the book. (Regarding some of the fine points, the rules change from youngsters' ball to high school to college to the pros. Check with your coach and learn the rules at your level of play.)

Here are some basic definitions:

Kickoffs: At the start of each half, and after every score, one team kicks off to the other (see pages 256-259).

Offense and Defense: The *offense* is the team with the ball, the *defense* the team without the ball. After receiving a kickoff or getting the ball in *any* way, a team goes on offense.

Line of Scrimmage: A line, sideline to sideline, even with the tip of the ball before the offense starts a play.

Down: After the kickoff, the offense starts to run a series of plays, or pre-planned maneuvers to move the ball forward. Each play takes up one *down*. The offense has four downs to make ten yards, or it must surrender the ball to the other team.

Running Play: On a *running play*, or *run*, the offense tries to move the ball forward with one of its men carrying the ball.

Passing Play: On a *passing play*, or *pass*, the offense tries to move the ball by throwing it forward (*passing* it) from behind the line of scrimmage, one man to another.

First Down: If the offense makes ten yards or more, it earns a *first down:* four more downs to gain ten more yards.

Touchdown: If an offensive player has legal control of the ball either even with or across the goal line of the defense, he scores a touchdown, worth six points.

Extra Point: After scoring a touchdown, a team can try for an *extra point* or *conversion*. Usually this is done by *place kick* (see below). At some levels of football (especially many high schools), a team may elect to try for a *two-point conversion:* the offense starts on the three-yard line and has one play to try to cross the goal line, as on a touchdown.

Field Goal: A field goal is worth three points. It is also kicked with a *place kick* (see below).

Place Kick: One man *places* the ball on the ground, end first, and holds it lightly with one finger. His teammate tries to kick it between the uprights of the goal posts. On an extra point (after a touchdown), this is worth one point. On an ordinary offensive down, this is a field goal, worth three points.

Punt: If the offense comes up to its fourth down, and it is not close enough to the other team's goal line to try a field goal—probably it will *punt*. A punt is a type of kick; the kicker drops the ball through the air and kicks it before it hits the ground. A punt cannot score points. All it does is kick the ball an average of 40 or so yards downfield; when the other team takes over on offense, it will be that much farther away from scoring points.

Safety: If the defense downs an offensive player with the ball in his own end zone, the defense scores a *safety* (two points). After a safety, the team that was scored upon must kick off to the other team from its own 20-yard line.

Choosing A Position

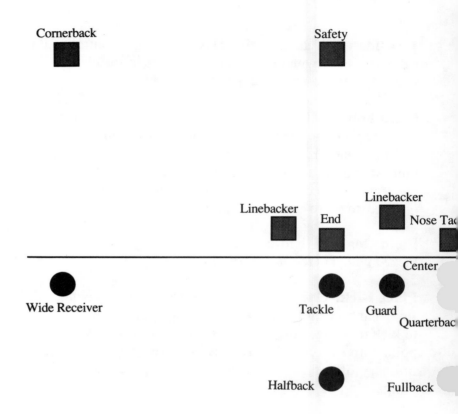

Cornerback

Safety

Linebacker

Linebacker

End

Nose Tac

Center

Wide Receiver

Tackle

Guard

Quarterbac

Halfback

Fullback

One thing I recommend to all young players is this: play as many different positions as you possibly can.

There are many different positions on a football field. They require athletes with many different qualities and skills. If you want to play badly enough, someplace you can find a position that suits you best.

One thing I recommend to all young players is this: play as many different positions as you can. Actually, if you possibly can, in practices and scrimmages try to play every position there is. The more positions you play, the better you will understand the game. The more you understand, the better you can play.

I've read that Ray Berry, the coach of the New England Patriots, has all of his wide receivers play defensive back for a day or two. They even go to the defensive back meetings.

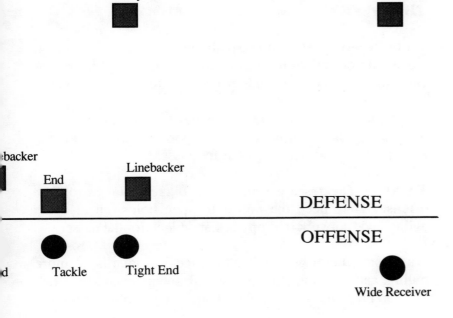

Safety

Cornerback

backer

Linebacker

End

DEFENSE

OFFENSE

Tackle

Tight End

Wide Receiver

d

I think that's smart. If you play defensive back a little bit, you get to know how they think. You learn what their responsibilities are—what they have to worry about. Knowing all that can help you as a wide receiver. The same thing is true of offensive and defensive linemen, of linebackers and running backs. And I know that playing defensive back and linebacker when I was younger helped me to play quarterback as I grew up. So move yourself around on the field.

There's one more advantage to playing a number of different positions. You will have a better chance to play. If your first choice is defensive back but you know how to play wide receiver, that gives you another opportunity to get out on the field instead of watching from the sidelines.

41

The more positions you play, the better you will understand the game. The more you understand, the better you can play.

THE OFFENSE

Wide Receiver: He can be small, and it's great if he's fast. He should definitely have good agility, and good hands for catching the ball (good hands can come through practice).

Tight End: He needs good size to make the important blocks on running plays, but he also needs good hands for catching and, hopefully, speed, to go out for passes.

Tackles: Tackles are usually the biggest players on the offense. They need the power to open holes but also the agility and footwork to drop back and block for the passer.

Guards: Often a bit smaller than tackles, guards do more pulling and running. Up through high school even a smallish guy can play guard—if he plays hard, and can run and think.

Center: You want a tough, strong, responsible man at center. He handles the ball on every play, snapping it to the quarterback or passing it back to kickers. Plus, he has to huddle up the team and act as the quarterback for the line.

Quarterback: Size and speed aren't as important as agile feet and hands, and the intelligence to run a team. Also, the quarterback should work hard to make himself a good passer.

Halfback: A halfback can come in any size, but he is usually a fast and shifty type of runner. He should also be a good receiver, a good blocker, and if he can pass, that's great.

Fullback: Usually the bigger, stronger runner. He has to power for short yardage, and block for the halfback and the quarterback. If a strong fullback has speed, he'll run a lot.

DEFENSE

Ends: Ends are the quicker, faster defensive linemen—to rush the passer and chase end runs—but they must still be tough enough to battle the tackles and tight end on inside runs.

Tackles: Often the heaviest people on defense, tackles have to stop the inside runs, often against double-team blocking, and also get a powerful pass rush. For sheer love of contact, this is a great position. There's action every play.

Linebackers: Usually some of the best athletes on the team. They have to be big and strong enough to stop the run, quick and agile enough to drop back against passes, and smart enough to read the offense and react immediately.

Cornerbacks: They must be fast enough to cover wide receivers, but tough enough to come up and challenge the big blockers on a sweep. Sure tackling is a must.

Safeties: Safeties are often among the smallest men on the field. They must be fast, smart, outstanding tacklers and good ball hawks. They are the last line of defense.

KICKERS

Punter: Just about everybody on the team should try out for punter. Good punters come in all different shapes and sizes. You need a "fast knee," but after that it's just work— practice on form and work on leg strength. Poise is vital, but can be developed if the leg is there.

Place Kicker: Size and speed don't matter much. A good leg and consistency do. A background in soccer usually helps.

Equipment

When it comes to your equipment, remember: an ounce of prevention is worth a pound of cure.

In many sports, what you wear is mainly for decoration. Your uniform tells you which team you're on. But in football, what you wear is vital to both your performance and your safety. It's not just for show.

There are many different pieces of equipment. You'll need to get help from coaches and older players when you first try to choose it and put it all on. But here are a few comments:

Helmet: Get a good tight fit. The helmet shouldn't wobble around on your head. Ask a coach for help.

Face Mask: Wear a large, strong one—but be sure it doesn't hit the shoulder pads and keep you from looking back over your shoulder when you turn your head.

Mouth Guard: Wear one. It's usually mandatory.

Shoulder Pads: Offensive linemen, running backs and all defensive people should have big, sturdy pads. Quarterbacks and wide receivers may use smaller pads.

Thigh And Knee Pads: They fit in your pants. Wear them. Your legs take a hard pounding.

Hip Pads: These fit inside your pants at the waist, guarding your hips and the base of your spine. Very important.

Rib Pads: Optional, but I would wear them. In fact, I *did* wear them—after I once took a lick in the ribs. Quarterbacks especially need them, since they often get hit up high.

Other Options: Many players wear neck protectors (rubber rolls that fit near the neck) and protective knee braces. I'm for safety first, so try them. They can prevent serious injury.

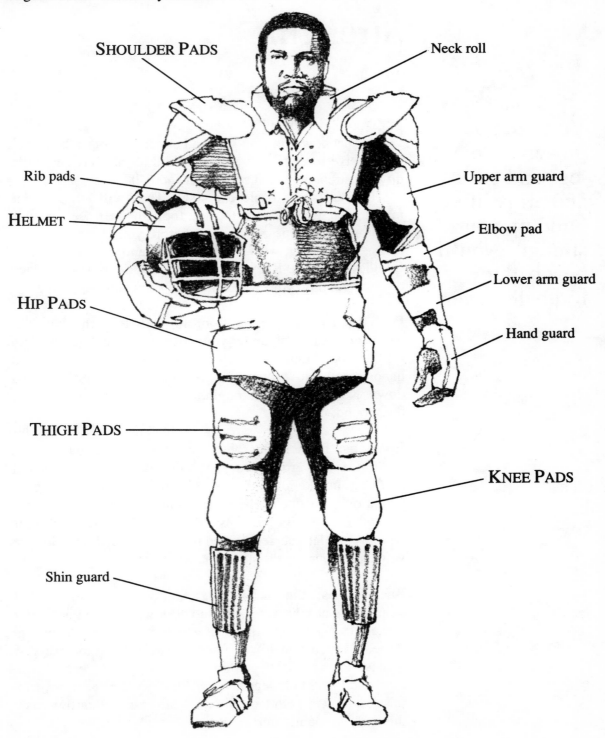

CAPITAL LETTERS = All players should wear these
Regular letters = Wear if you wish

SHOULDER PADS

Neck roll

Rib pads

Upper arm guard

HELMET

Elbow pad

Lower arm guard

HIP PADS

Hand guard

THIGH PADS

KNEE PADS

Shin guard

Strength

You need that power in your legs and back and arms. If you build up your strength, you'll be a better football player.

To play football well, you have to be strong. You need that power in your legs and back and arms—the explosive force to move quickly and hit hard. If you build up your strength, you'll be a better football player.

Here are some basic exercises. They will build up the major muscles you need to play football well. Be sure you warm up with some calisthenics before you start these exercises. Start easily, with a few of each, and do them at least five days a week. Keep a record of how many you do each day and put it on your wall. That will keep you improving.

Push-Ups: Lie flat on the floor on your stomach. Put your palms on the ground under your shoulders. Push yourself up off the ground until your arms are straight (only your toes and hands should now touch the ground). Push yourself up and down. Keep your back straight, and only touch your chest to the ground.

Roll-Ups: Trainers say these are better than regular sit-ups. Lie flat on the ground on your back. Bend your legs about halfway, but keep your feet flat on the ground. Put your hands on your chest. Lift your shoulders and back off the ground six or eight inches—then just hold two or three seconds and let yourself back down. Repeat. This should give you a good burn in the stomach muscles.

Back Raises: Lie flat on the ground on your stomach. Put your hands at your sides. Raise and lower one leg about six inches. Repeat a few times. Raise and lower the other leg. Repeat. Raise and lower your head and shoulders a few inches. Repeat. After you do back raises for a week or two, raise and lower both legs at once. Finally, after several weeks, raise and lower both legs and the head at once, starting to do this only gradually and easily.

Push-Ups

Roll-Ups

Back Raises

Leg-Ups

Do these exercises (or any exercises) only after consulting with your parents and with your doctor. Safety first.

Leg-Ups: Find something to step up onto (no more than 18 inches high). Put your right foot up. Raise yourself up with your right leg (doing a little jump with your toes at the top), then let yourself back down onto your left leg again. Do this repeatedly with the right leg, then with the left leg. Hold onto something sturdy with one hand, to keep your balance.

CAUTION: Do these exercises (or any exercises) only after consulting with your parents and with your doctor. Safety first. Many high school teams now have weight-lifting programs. Be sure your doctor approves, and NEVER lift weights except under the watchful eye of a trained adult.

Flexibility

If you want to stretch a muscle, the thing to do is stretch it out and just hold the position for 20 or 30 seconds. Don't strain hard. Just stretch out until you feel it pull a bit (no pain) and then hold.

Strength is important. But so is flexibility. Your muscles have to stretch out easily so you can make the moves you need on the field. If your muscles aren't loose, you'll get pulls and sprains. Flexibility keeps you healthy.

In the past few years, experts have found out a lot about how to stretch your muscles best. Say you want to touch your toes. In the old days we reached down for our toes and then bounced up and down a few inches over and over. We thought we were stretching the muscles out. Actually, it turns out that bouncing the muscle just tightens it up. If you want to stretch a muscle, the thing to do is stretch it out and just hold the position for 20 or 30 seconds. Don't strain. Just stretch out until you feel it pull a bit (no pain) and then hold. This is called *static stretching—static* because you don't move.

Here are six static stretching exercises. Do them just before playing. (Be sure to warm up before stretching, using light calisthenics):

1. The Jacknife: Keep legs straight. Bend at hip joint and keep your back absolutely straight. Keep head up. Reach out for ground in front of you. The goal is to stretch the legs, not the back. Don't strain. Don't force. Reach as far as you can easily, then hold for 20-30 seconds.

2. The Bridge: Reach down to ground with hips at 90° angle. Keep head up and arms and legs straight. Press shoulders toward feet. Get comfortable, then stretch heels down toward ground (without straining).

3. The Bow: Put right foot back and kneel down. Let right knee trail back and put weight on left leg. Left knee should bend 45°. Arch back backward. Hold for 20-30 seconds, then reverse legs.

4. The Twist: Sit down with left leg out straight. Lift right leg over left, with knee bent. Lock left arm against right side of right leg. Reach back with right hand and twist head and shoulders around as far as comfortable. Keep back straight up. Hold for 20-30 seconds, then reverse.

5. The Fountain: Sit on heels. Reach back with arms and arch back. If it's easy, stretch backward enough to put weight on elbows, not hands.

6. The Warrior: Spread your legs. Slowly bend your left leg. Keep your left toe pointed straight to the left and your left knee back over your foot. Stretch your right leg out. Keep your right foot flat and pointed forward at 45°. Hold 20-30 seconds, then reverse legs.

The Jacknife

The Bridge

Before starting these stretching exercises, always warm up with a few minutes of light calisthenics—jumping jacks, windmilling arms, jogging in place, etc.

The Bow

The Twist

The Fountain

The Warrior

Endurance

It's a terrible feeling to be better than the other guy, to be whipping him all day—and then lose your drive.

You win football games in the fourth quarter. The team that's strong in that last period is the team that will get the job done. That's why you have to build up your wind—to get some endurance. It's a bad feeling to be better than the other guy, to whip him all day, then get to that last quarter—and lose your drive. I think Vince Lombardi said it best: "Fatigue makes cowards of us all."

Think about the *kind* of endurance you need to play this game. Cross-country running is a good sport—but remember: football players run short distances—often less than ten yards per play, and almost never more than 40. So do a lot of short sprint work as well.

You have to work at it. But that's no reason it can't be some fun, why you can't make a game out of it and keep yourself interested. Here are some drills that will do the trick:

Long Bomb Sprints: Get with a friend or two. One guy goes straight out long, while his buddy throws a pass to him. After doing the throwing, the passer sprints down to join the other guys. Turn around, another guy throws, and do the same thing coming back. Have fun with this drill.

Quick Sprints: Get down in your stance. Sprint ten yards all-out. Stop before you go another ten yards. Get down in your stance and go again. Keep it up. Try to beat your buddies. Vary it by sprinting backwards, or sideways, or start from your stance and *pull* right or left (see page 108).

Cut 'Em Off At The Pass (see diagram): Get out on a football field with a buddy or two. Take turns playing runner and defensive back. The runner starts closer to the sideline and the defender starts farther downfield. The runner tries to outrun the defensive back down the sideline. The defender gets practice taking the correct angle of pursuit.

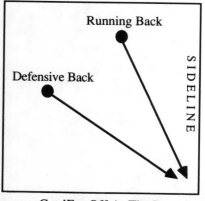

Cut 'Em Off At The Pass

A football game is going to wear you out and leave you looking used up. But late in the fourth quarter, when games are won or lost, you've got to be ready to go for it one more time.

Agility

When you do agility drills, don't just do them to get tired. Focus on being as quick and graceful as you can.

Playing football, you have to get yourself out of the strangest spots and over the wildest piles. To play the game well, you have to be agile.

A guy I think of is "The Refrigerator," William Perry. He weighs more than 300 pounds, but I've seen him jump up and down off a table—both feet at *once*. John Riggins is another good example. He's a big fullback, but he's also very agile. I used to see him work on it. One thing he did was to skip rope a lot, to give himself quick feet. He'd also punch a speed bag, the type boxers use, to speed up his hands.

Both of those drills could help you, too. I'll list several others here, and there are three shown in the photos on the following page. A good agility exercise also helps you build up your endurance. But when you do one, don't just do it to get tired. Focus on being as quick and graceful as you can.

Quick Jacks: You've probably done jumping jacks. Here's a good variation. Have somebody call out, "Hop!" and hop your legs open sideways as fast as you can. Pop your hands up to your helmet at the same time. Then the same guy hollers, "Close!" and you snap both feet back together and bring your hands down. Keep going: "Hop! Close! Hop! Close!" and react to his voice as fast as you can each time. You can also do this moving your feet forward and back. It's a good drill to work on reactions and footwork.

All Fours: Drop down so your weight is on both hands and both feet. Using quick, short motions, run forward, backward, left and right, staying on all fours.

Quick Around: Run ten yards straight, drop one hand to the ground, run in a quick circle with that hand down, then run back. For a Figure Eight Quick Around drill, see photo opposite.

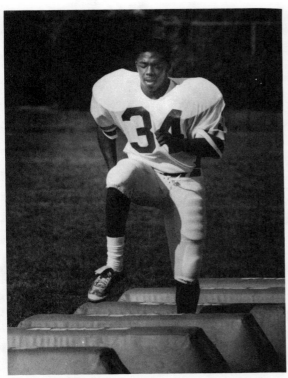

Practice high-stepping—over tires, ropes, or dummies. High knee action helps break tackles and helps you when you need to step over fallen bodies.

Three players run the Figure Eight Quick Around. Run between two spots ten yards apart, and turn quickly around the spot with hand on the ground.

After hitting the sled, roll off quickly toward the ground.

Roll over and bounce back up into a good hitting position.

Hit next dummy. Use this good form—back straight, head up, feet spread.

When you see a
really fast runner,
you will always see
that his toes are
pointed way back
as they leave the
ground. That is
because he has used
his foot to throw
the ground back
and drive himself
forward.

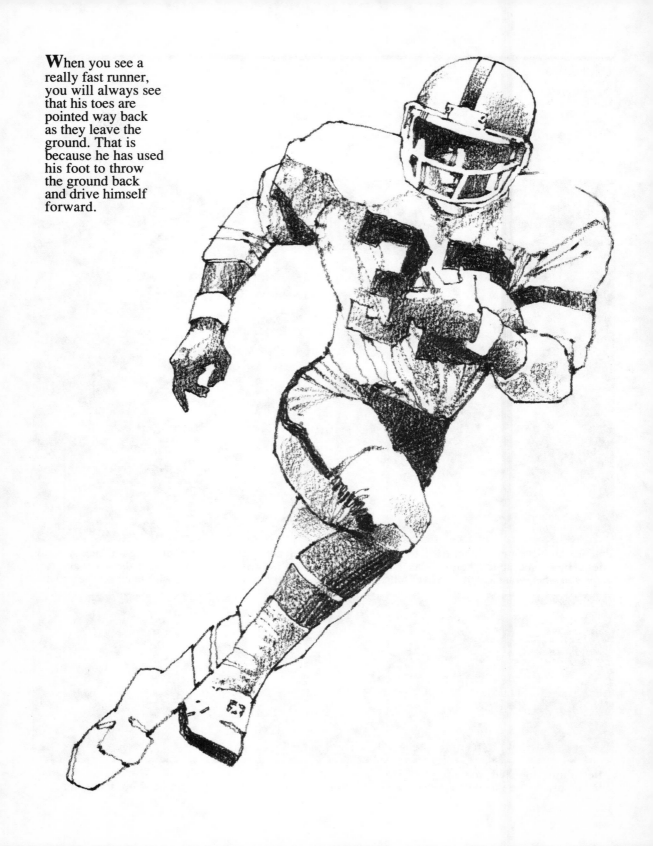

Speed

Most people think that speed is something you're born with. You either have it or you don't. There's nothing you can do about it. Well, that isn't true. There's a lot you can do to increase your speed. We teach running techniques every year at our football camp.

When most children want to run, they just start moving everything. They get their arms and legs moving, and everything is flying every which way. The heart is there, the desire is there. But they don't know how to translate that desire into the most direct, efficient motion. They don't know how to get everything going in the right direction, with no wasted effort.

If I were you, I'd put a lot of time into learning how to run as fast as possible. Study what we say here. Spend time every spring with a track coach (Mike Haynes, the All-Pro corner-back with the Los Angeles Raiders, still works with a track coach every year; he's in his 30s and faster now than he was as a rookie). The more people you can outrun, the better.

Driving Off: According to many track coaches, the biggest failing of a slow man is that he doesn't drive hard with his calf muscle, he doesn't push off with his toes. A real sprinter's foot flies up behind him. Why? Because he has flipped the ground behind him with his toes—and done it so hard his foot flies up. By really *throwing* that ground back, you drive yourself forward. You fly through the air much farther on each step. That's why we say of a fast guy, "Wow, he's really *flying*." To learn to do this, you need to practice. But, hey, if Mike Haynes can still practice sprinting techniques after being an All-Pro, so can you.

Body Lean: A fast man keeps his upper body leaning forward a bit. Not a lot at full stride, but just enough to keep his weight out front and pulling him along.

> According to many track coaches, the biggest failing of a slow man is that he doesn't drive hard with his calf muscle, he doesn't push off with his toes.

55

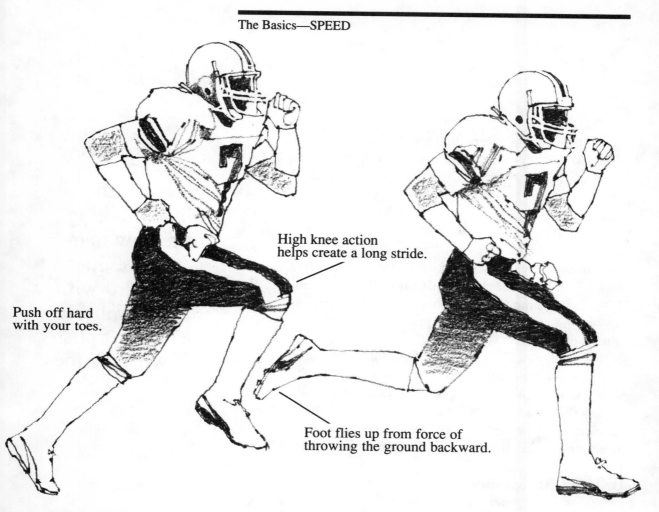

High knee action helps create a long stride.

Push off hard with your toes.

Foot flies up from force of throwing the ground backward.

Use a high knee action, reach way out in front of yourself with your foot, and use a smooth arm action.

High Knee Action: After your foot throws the ground backward, you want to bring your leg forward with a nice, high knee action. This helps lengthen your stride, so you fly farther on each step.

Long Reach: After you get your knee nice and high, then reach way out with your front leg. Get a good, long stride, and land on your toes, not your heel.

Smooth, Straight Arm Action: Don't let your arms fly around. Use them. Pump them for rhythm in a short, straight motion. Practice by putting your hand next to your waist, then pumping up next to your jaw and back to your waist. That

56

Keep body leaning forward from the waist, with shoulders slightly hunched.

Arm action is simple, short, up-and-down stroke. Keep elbow bent. Don't let arm flop or wave around loosely.

Drive hard again with your toes

short, straight arc is just what you want to give you a good rhythm without wasting a lot of motion.

Relax Your Hands And Jaw: It will take you a while to think about all these parts of your stride, practice each part, and then put it all back together. It may take a few months, but it will be worth it the first time you dust off a guy who used to beat you. Then, when you are running with a simple and powerful style, there is one more thing track coaches suggest. Relax. To do that, they say, relax your hands and your jaw. Don't make a tight fist and don't clench your teeth. By relaxing your hands and jaw, the whole body relaxes. You usually become about a tenth of a second faster at 40 yards.

The Hitting Position

If you watch the pros play, you'll see they usually move around low to the ground, like a tiger waiting to pounce. That's the basic hitting position.

If you watch kids play football, you'll see that a lot of them run around carelessly, just like they do on the playground at lunchtime. But if you watch the pros play, you'll see they usually move around low to the ground, crouched and ready like a tiger waiting to pounce.

That's the basic *hitting position.* It's usually the stance that linebackers line up in—and most defensive players, plus blockers and runners, move around in it most of the time. A pro is always ready to hit or be hit. You should be, too.

Legs: Spread your feet comfortably—just wider than the shoulders. Keep your weight evenly distributed on the balls of your feet. Bend your knees and "sit down." If you stand up straight-legged, you can't push and drive.

Body: Bend forward at the waist. Crouch down as low as you can and still see what you need. Keep your back ramrod straight—so the drive from your legs can go straight ahead.

Head: Keep your head UP! Keep it tipped back, with neck muscles bunched up. You must *see* to play. Every second, every play, every game, KEEP YOUR HEAD UP!

Feet are just wider than shoulders, arms out and ready. Knees are bent near right angle, so is waist. Keep your head UP.

In the hitting position, you are coiled up, ready to attack. Your feet are spread (usually about shoulder width), your knees and waist are bent, your back is straight and your head is up. In the hitting position you should be intense, ready for action, ready to explode.

Stance and Start

Every play of every game begins with the stance and start. You should practice your stance and start every day.

Your stance and start really make a big difference. Well begun is half done. If you have a good stance and a good start, you can explode in any direction. If you don't have a good stance, it's like you're stuck in the mud. It's hard to get yourself moving.

Too many boys don't have a good stance—and therefore they use wasted motion going from point A to point B. Because their stance is bad, they have to regroup their weight before they can take off. For example, maybe you get your weight too far out front on your hand. The only place you can go right now is straight ahead. To pull left or right is a big problem—you have to push off with your hand, get your weight together, then start out. That's too slow. Football is usually a race—and you can't afford to lose. You need a good stance.

If you are an offensive player, you also can't afford to change your stance all the time. You can't line up one way to charge straight ahead and another way to pull out. That just tells the defense what you are doing. You might as well wear a sign saying, "I'm going to pull right." The defense loves to get such a tip. The best advantage the offense has is surprise. If you change your stance and give away your surprise, they're going to beat you. Maybe an offensive lineman puts his weight forward on his hand on a running play, then back on his heels on a pass. He's tipping the defense. He's giving the play away. Football is tough enough without giving the other guy such a big advantage.

There are many different stances on a football field—because of the many different responsibilities the various positions have. Linebackers and defensive backs often use the basic hitting position (see previous page). Offensive linemen, defensive linemen and offensive backs often use a stance like Number 79 on the page at right. Other stances are shown on the next page and elsewhere in this book.

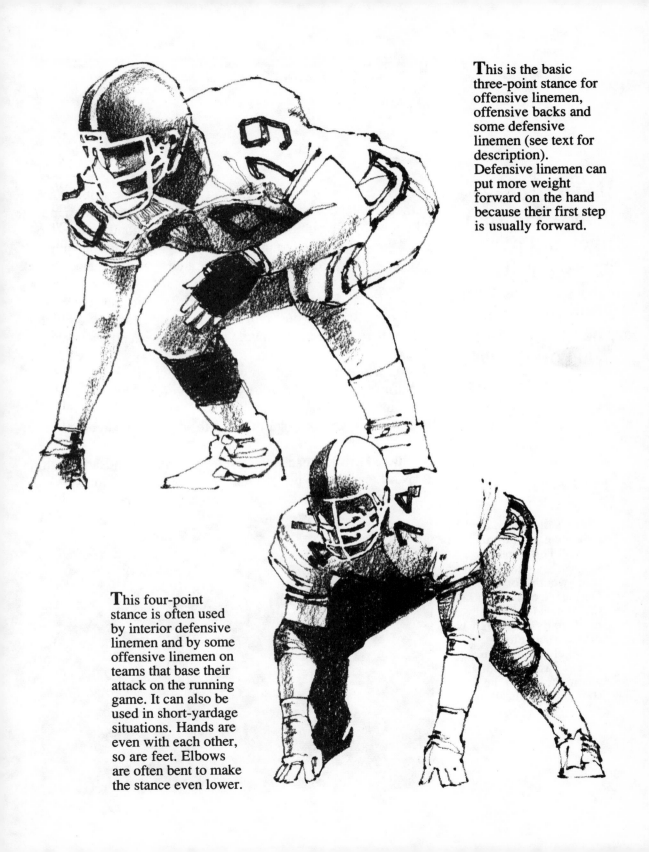

This is the basic three-point stance for offensive linemen, offensive backs and some defensive linemen (see text for description). Defensive linemen can put more weight forward on the hand because their first step is usually forward.

This four-point stance is often used by interior defensive linemen and by some offensive linemen on teams that base their attack on the running game. It can also be used in short-yardage situations. Hands are even with each other, so are feet. Elbows are often bent to make the stance even lower.

Practice your stance and start over and over and over. They can give you an advantage on every play.

Here is a good routine for getting into the basic three-point stance (the stance of Number 79 on the previous page). Do it like this, by the numbers, until it becomes second nature. Go ahead and call out the numbers as you go through the steps. (Reverse the words *right* and *left* for a left-handed stance).

1. Set Feet. Spread your feet slightly wider than your shoulders. Stagger your right foot back so the toe is even with somewhere between the middle of the left foot and the heel.

2. Squat Down. Bend your knees and place elbows or forearms on knees. Put your weight comfortably on the balls of your feet. (You should get used to this "up" position; occasionally you may start from it to surprise the defense.)

3. Place Hand. Reach out with your right hand and lean forward until it hits the ground. Balance on your knuckles or fingertips. Carry more weight on legs, less on hand.

Here is the stance used by defensive ends to rush the passer. This is nearly a sprinter's stance—with most weight forward. Defensive ends often favor this stance (unless they are head-up over an offensive lineman), and they definitely use it in an all-out pass-rush situation, where they want the fastest start straight ahead.

62

To get a good start, first get a good stance: back straight, head up.

Drive hard with the legs, with both thigh muscles and calf muscles.

Keep body low and drive hard. Pump the arms and keep head up.

4. Raise Head And Flatten Back. Imagine a drawstring from the top of your head to the base of your spine. Pull this string up taut. Your eyes must be up as high as possible—and your back so flat it would make a good table.

Use a similar routine to get into any other stance. Ask for a coach's help to get it perfect.

To get a good, fast start, follow these tips:

Explode With Your Legs: Your thigh muscles and calf muscles must go off like dynamite. Explode! The first three steps should be all-out driving—don't forget to use the toes.

Stay Low: Don't stand up. Drive straight ahead, with back straight. Keep your weight low and your body out in front of your legs, where it will pull you forward. Drive hard. If you keep your mind focused on driving, your body will do it.

Keep Your Head UP: Your back is straight, but your head is tipped back so you can see. In football you always want to know what's going on up ahead. Keep your head UP.

Leverage

Keep your feet spread out shoulder width and driving. You get your power and your balance from a good wide base.

Drive straight into your man. Hit just under his pads with your shoulder. Then bang upwards into his chest with your forearm. Keep your head up. If your head goes down, so will you. If your head stays up, you'll drive him up. Also, keep your feet spread shoulder width. The most common mistake of the young player is to get his feet right next to each other. With your feet too close together, anybody can knock you over sideways. Keep your feet spread out shoulder width for balance and stability.

Leverage is one secret to success on the football field. It makes the small man mighty. If you lever a man up in the air so he can't drive with his legs, you've *got* him.

The basic way to get leverage is with your shoulder and forearm. Bang the guy just under his pads with your shoulder, and drive your forearm hard up into his chest. Keep your back straight, your head up—*and your feet spread out shoulder width and driving hard.*

Don't aim downward to get under him. He'll simply push you down. Drive straight at him. He'll usually come up a bit, and when you hit him under his pads, his own momentum will run him upward, like a car running up a hill. Then lever him up—with your feet shoulder width and driving.

PHOTO: LOU WITT

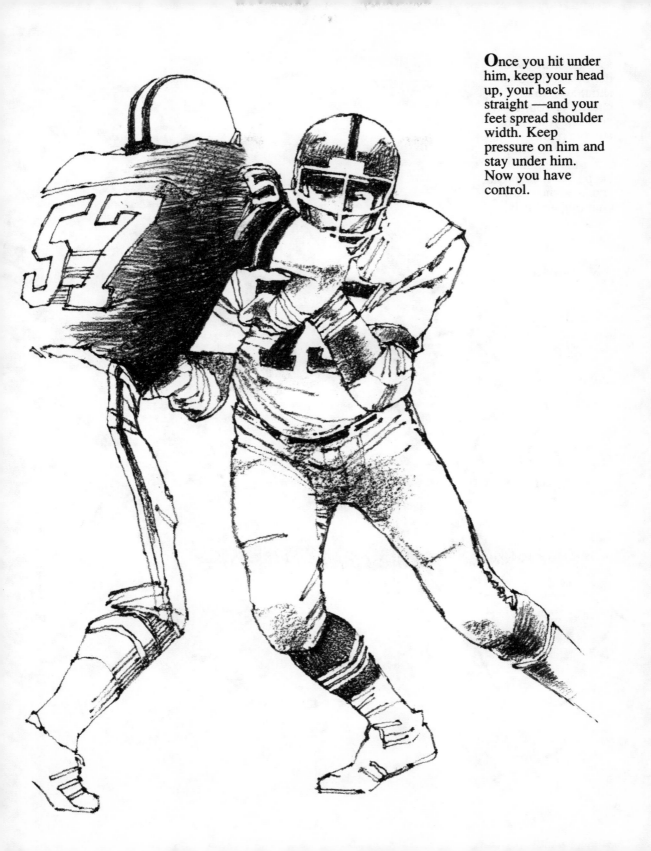

Once you hit under him, keep your head up, your back straight —and your feet spread shoulder width. Keep pressure on him and stay under him. Now you have control.

On the basic shoulder block, drive your shoulder into his chest. Put your head between your man and the runner—and keep your head up. After the first hit, keep your feet spread, and keep them always churning and driving.

The Basic Shoulder Block

You can't talk about the basics of football without talking about blocking and tackling. After all, football is a game of hitting. Hall-of-Fame coach Vince Lombardi said it clearly: "Football is not a contact sport. Dancing is a contact sport. Football is a *collision* sport." The team that wins the collisions is the team that wins the games.

There are basic techniques to win these battles. We'll start with blocking—the basic shoulder block. Later we'll get into other types of blocks.

Blocking takes more technique than tackling. A blocker has to be concerned with technique every second. Sometimes a tackler just grabs onto something any which way and holds on for dear life. But a blocker always has to keep good form. Good blockers are *made*, not born. If you work on it, you can be a good blocker.

The shoulder block is the most basic block in football. The idea of the shoulder block is to blast straight out into your man, lever him up—and at the same time, turn yourself to get your back facing the hole.

Here are some tips on how to throw the shoulder block:

Fire Straight Out: Keep your back straight and level. "You explode into your man on a horizontal plane," says Mike Kenn, an All-Pro offensive tackle for the Atlanta Falcons. If you are aimed downward as you hit, you will nose dive. This is the worst thing that can happen to a blocker, crashing to the ground. On the other hand, if you stand straight up as you hit, the other guy will get under you. That's no good either. So "explode into him on a horizontal plane"—and hit with your shoulder. Which shoulder? The rule is to keep your head and body between your opponent and the runner.

Keep Your Head Up: You may be surprised how often I tell you to keep your head up. Well, I'll tell you what. You

> Blocking takes more technique than tackling. A blocker has to be concerned with technique every second.

Always keep your feet as wide as they were in your stance. Always keep a good, wide base underneath you.

can't say it too often. So many players duck their head down when hitting. It's just terrible. First, you can't see. Second, if your head goes down, *you* go down. You just collapse on the ground. Third, with your neck bent over, you might get hurt. So keep your head up. Coaches tell blockers, "Look up and you'll drive your man up." (Keep your head up, but remember: don't *hit* with your head. It's illegal.)

Don't Overhit: Hit your man hard enough to stop him. Explode with your legs, hit hard with your shoulder, and flip your forearm hard up into his chest (some coaches call this the "flipper"). Hit hard, but keep yourself *under control*. Never collapse to the ground. To get a good block, you have to hit him—and then *stay* with him. To stay with him, you should keep your feet shoulder spread width and driving hard. One tip: don't take a big first step. "Keep your first step a very short one," says Atlanta's Kenn, "not more than a foot."

Keep Your Feet Wide: You should always keep your feet as wide as they were in your stance. Always keep a good, wide base underneath you. Says Dan Dierdorf, for years

A lot of blockers lunge out too far on the first blow. You have to hit your man a good shot and stop him, but don't lose control.

If you overstride, then your weight is too far forward and you fall down. Use short steps and keep your feet shoulder width for good balance.

Once you have the block started, keep driving into his chest. You have to keep your feet spread, and keep them constantly moving and driving to keep the block going.

"A lot of guys can hit a good first blow," says Dierdorf. "But then they're through. Their block is over. But a good blocker keeps those feet moving all the time."

an All-Pro lineman with the St. Louis Cardinals, "If you get your feet close together, the guy can hit you in the shoulder and knock you over like a telephone pole."

Keep Your Feet Driving: Don't just lean up against your guy. Keep your feet chopping and driving. Keep your feet moving all the time. "A lot of guys can hit a good first blow," says Dierdorf. "But then they're through. Their block is over. But a good blocker keeps those feet moving all the time." Sooner or later, the defensive guy has to raise up and look for the ball carrier. *"That's* when you get him," Kenn says. "If you're still in a good position and your feet are still driving, you can turn even a bad block into a good one."

Turn Your Back To The Hole: If you want to open a hole on your left, hit your man with your right shoulder. Get your head between him and the hole. After you hit him and stop his momentum, then you can swing your hips around until your back is facing the hole. Now you are between your man and the hole—in a good, basic hitting position. By the time he can get by you, the ball carrier should be gone.

Once you get a block started, be sure to keep your feet wide so you always have a good base. Also, keep your feet moving. Keep driving. A good blocker is one who sticks to his block.

After you make your first hit, then you can swing your hips around so your back faces the hole your runner will run through (Number 74 here is swinging around to his left). Even if you don't drive your man back very far, this places you right in his way.

This is a classic tackle.
The tackler is hitting
hard with his shoulder
and is "hitting on the
rise"— driving his man
upward. He has his
head in front and has
kept his head up. He
has wrapped his arms
around and grabbed on
to the runner. When
you have the chance,
this is the form you
want.

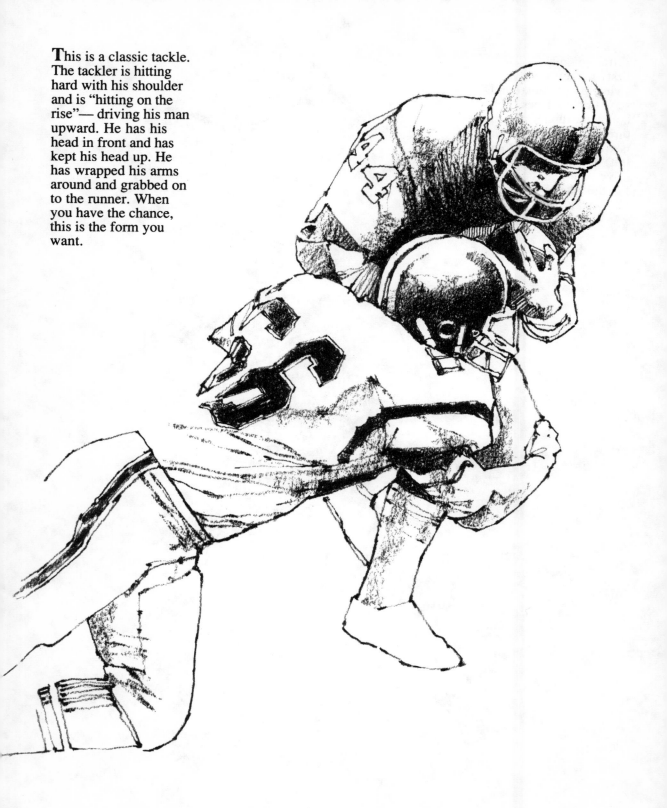

Tackling

If you want to play defense, you have to tackle people. Every last man on defense has to be a good tackler. Broken tackles give up yards and points.

I got hurt once in the pros trying to make a tackle. This was in the pre-season, and our fullback fumbled the ball. I hurt my knee trying to tackle the guy and missed most of the season. People asked me, "Why did you try to make that tackle? It was only a pre-season game." And that made me pretty mad. I mean, I was out there playing in a *football* game. If some guy is trying to run past you and score a touchdown, you tackle him, that's all. How would you feel if one of your teammates stood there and watched some guy go by with the ball? I know how I'd feel. I'd tell the jerk to get the heck off the field if he didn't want to play.

There are many ways to make a tackle. Maybe you're falling down, some guy is trying to throw a block on you —and here comes the runner. *Tackle* him! I don't care how. *Get* him. You can't always get a perfect form tackle, but you have to get that guy down. That's why desire is vital for a tackler. As George Allen says, "A great tackler has a burning desire to bring the runner down." Desire is not always enough, though, without technique. If you're ready to hit people, here are some tips:

Get In A Good Hitting Position: If you have a chance, get coiled and ready to attack. If you have run some distance, try in the last steps to "break down"—get under control and settle into the hitting position. Keep your head UP!

Focus Your Eyes On A Definite Target: If the man is running toward you, focus on his belt buckle. Then drive your shoulder right there. Don't ever look up at the runner's head. He can fake with his head and eyes and fool you. But his body goes where his belt buckle goes.

> Maybe you're falling down, some guy is trying to block you—and here comes the runner. *Tackle* him! I don't care how. *Get* him. Desire is vital for a tackler.

73

You may have your arms around him, but still he drags you for two, three, even four yards. You can't have that. Keep your legs driving.

To make a tackle, get in a good hitting position and burn your eyes right into his belt buckle.

Keep Your Eyes Open: Just when most young tacklers are about to hit the runner, they close their eyes. It's natural, but it's not good. "If the runner cuts at the last second," says Karl Mecklenburg, Denver Bronco All-Pro linebacker, "you'll never know where he went. Keep your eyes open."

Drive Hard With Your Shoulder: Really pop the guy. Don't just reach out with your arms and grab at him. Bang him with your shoulder—and drive *through* him.

Get Your Head In Front: If you are coming from the side, get your head in front of him to cut him off. "Get your head across his bow," says Mecklenburg. "If only your arm is in front of the runner, he may break through."

Grab Something: As you pop him, close your arms around him. Now grab something. "It doesn't matter what you get," Mecklenburg says, "some jersey, a pad, even your own wrist. Hold on for dear life. A good tackler has very strong hands."

Keep Your Legs Driving: Many tacklers hit, grab—and then go limp. They just fall down and try to drag the runner down. But a good runner is going to keep his legs driving and drag you for two, three, even four yards. You can't have that. Those extra yards may be the first down. So anytime you tackle a guy, even from the side, keep your legs driving. Fight the guy. Try not to give up one more inch.

Be Smart: If you have a chance, you'll hit different guys in different places. On a big runner, you may go low. If you hit him high, he'll just take you for a ride. But on a small, tricky guy, you want to hit high. If you go down and try to chase his feet, he'll skip them around and you'll get nothing but air. Thinking helps a tackler like everybody else.

As a good tackler comes up to the runner, he keeps his eyes glued to the runner's belt buckle. That's the target. Hit it hard with your shoulder.

If you are going after a big guy, you may want to hit him low. If you hit high he can carry you, but if you hit low, you can knock his feet out from under him. Your choice will depend on your position as the runner arrives. The main thing is to get him any way you can.

You may not get a classic form tackle that often, but this is what you want. Back straight, head up, arms locked around. On a perfect tackle you dip your hips (not your head) just before striking and "hit on the rise." If you can hit upwards, you lift the runner and prevent him from using his legs to drive. Remember: hit with your shoulder and *do not "spear" with your head*. It is illegal and very dangerous to hit with your head.

PART TWO

The
Running
Game

The Running Game

Every smart coach and quarterback loves the running game. If you can run the ball, then things are comfortable. You have control of the game. You just take it right at the defense and move down the field. You still pass the ball, but you pass when *you* want to. They aren't expecting the pass. You have time to throw. Things are easier.

I remember a couple of times in my career when the running game was just awesome. Once was down at Alabama. We were playing Tulane when I was a sophomore. Coach Bryant came to me before the game and told me, "Joe, I want you to throw that ball more than you ever have in your life. I don't care if you throw it 20 times." Now you have to understand: throwing 20 times for Coach Bryant in 1962 would be like throwing it 60 times today. So we went out there, rolled up and down and beat Tulane 44-6—and I threw only six passes all night. I couldn't see calling many passes with things going that comfortably. I'll never forget Coach Bryant after the game. He just chuckled. He knew I took what we could get.

My point is, when you get that running game going, life is easier. It's the simplest way to win football games. You just keep putting it to them, you chew up yards, you score some points—and you use up the clock. There are no incomplete passes to stop the clock, so you use up the clock while their offense has to sit on the bench. It's hard for them to score when they don't get much time with the ball.

The running game is really a team effort. All 11 guys have to work together. Everybody but the runner (and sometimes the quarterback) has to throw a good block. And it all has to be coordinated, the line blocking with the runner's timing and so on. It's not easy to do right. It takes a lot of practice, working together. But when you can get that running game going during a game, when you cruise up and down the field and just push the defense around, it makes it all worth it.

The Quarterback

The quarterback has an important role in the running game. He needs to understand the attack—he should know why to run certain plays against certain defenses. He also has a physical job to do—he must make a flawless handoff at the right exchange point at the right time, or he must pitch the ball out precisely.

Also the quarterback may be a running threat himself. He should master the skills of a running back. If you want to play quarterback, you should study the pages later in this section on how to run the ball.

In this section, we will talk about the basic quarterback job in the running game—taking the ball from center and getting it to the runner. It seems pretty simple. But there are fine points of technique you should know really well.

The Mental Checklist: The first thing I tell every young quarterback is this: have a mental checklist when you come out of the huddle. We've talked about this already. When you come out of that huddle, you don't want to be thinking about pizza after the game—or that giant nose tackle on the defense. You want to be thinking about *exactly* what you are going to do.

On every running play, I tell the quarterback to have this four-point checklist (you'd have a different checklist on a pass play). As you leave the huddle, first repeat the snap count to yourself. Second, visualize in your mind exactly where you are going to give the ball to the runner—we call this spot the "exchange point," the point where the ball changes hands. Third, visualize the step or steps you will take to get to that exchange point. Finally, repeat the snap count in your mind. Now when the center snaps you the ball, you aren't surprised and confused. You know exactly what to do—and you do it. The mental checklist is one of the most important techniques in football.

> The first thing I tell every young quarterback is this: have a mental checklist when you come out of the huddle. You want to know *exactly* what you are going to do.

83

NANCY HOGUE

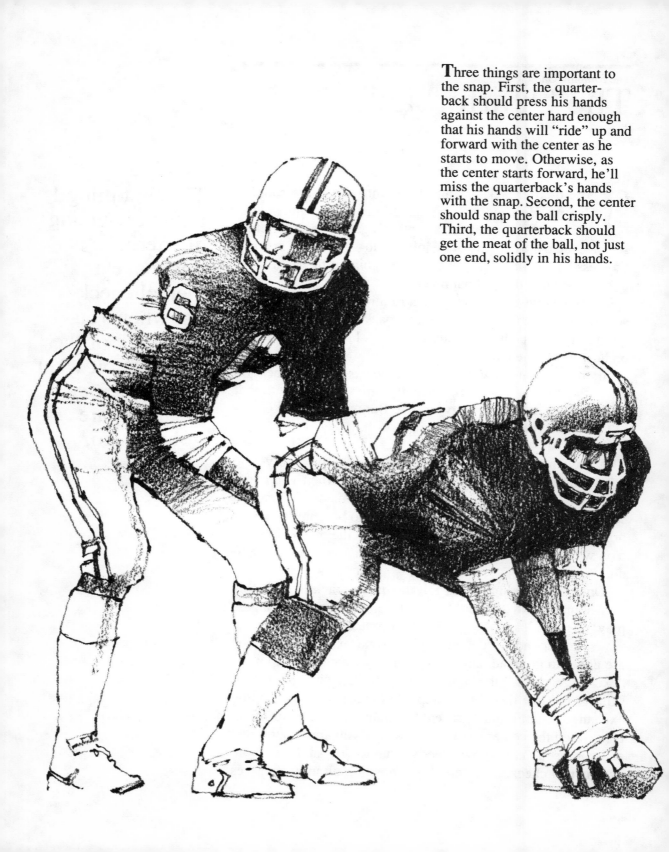

Three things are important to the snap. First, the quarterback should press his hands against the center hard enough that his hands will "ride" up and forward with the center as he starts to move. Otherwise, as the center starts forward, he'll miss the quarterback's hands with the snap. Second, the center should snap the ball crisply. Third, the quarterback should get the meat of the ball, not just one end, solidly in his hands.

The Snap

Every play begins with the snap of the ball. When the snap is between the center and the quarterback, it should be nearly automatic. I say "nearly" because Mother Nature can make that ball slippery sometimes. And it's a sad joke how the quarterback or center can sometimes forget the snap count. I've been out on the field in front of 80,000 people with no idea in the *world*. I forgot my mental checklist. You just have to grab your center and ask him.

As to the snap itself, you should work on it until both you and the center are confident and comfortable. In my 13 pro years we only missed one snap—and that was one too many.

The center starts in the stance you see here. His legs are fairly wide. His back is absolutely straight and his head up. Next he wants to roll the ball and get the laces in the right position. For a right-handed center, this usually means putting the laces slightly to the left as you grab it. You want to hit the laces into the quarterback's passing hand as you snap.

The quarterback takes a comfortable, upright stance, with feet shoulder width and knees bent. Put your weight comfortably on the balls of your feet. Keep your upper body straight as you can so you can look out and see the whole defense.

You should work on the snap until both the quarterback and the center are confident and comfortable.

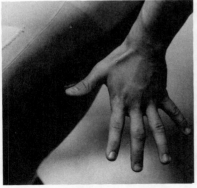

One style: passing hand is up, other hand spreads left. Thumbs are together. Ball is snapped sideways.

A different style: both hands on top. Center snaps with both hands, aiming tip of ball at QB.

85

Keep the ball in and protected as you pivot away from center. Hold it right against your stomach where it's harder for the defense to see—and harder for one of your linemen or backs to knock out of your hands.

The Pivot

Once you've got the ball from the center, pull it right back against your stomach (see illustration). Then each step you take is very precise. Your coach should show you each and every step you take to reach the correct exchange point (handoff spot) by the most direct route.

You need to pivot around to get started—at least one quarter of the way around, and sometimes a big three-quarters turn. I find that turning my head and getting my eyes on the target helps my body get going in the right direction. Turn your head and eyes quickly to where you have to go. The rest of you will follow. Even if you have to pivot nearly *all* the way around, first whip that head around. Burn those eyes right to the runner and the spot where you are going. Your body will go with you almost by itself.

To help you pivot quickly, do two things. First, "sit down" just a bit as you whip your head around. Drop your rear end. This will get you moving. At the same time, pull hard with the elbow and hip that have to do the turning. Whip that elbow and hip around, too, and stay down low in a "hitting position" to maintain good balance. It's really an easy move. Do it 15 or 20 times and you'll get it.

> Turn your head and eyes quickly to where you have to go. The rest of you will follow.

Be in a good high stance, with your feet spread shoulder width and your knees bent comfortably.

Pull the ball back into you stomach. Whip your head and eyes around to get your body turning.

Stay down with knees bent. Keep the ball close to your body until it is actually time to hand off.

One type of pocket to receive the handoff: the inside arm (the arm nearest the quarterback) is up high and horizontal, while the other hand is down next to the stomach to keep the ball from going through.

The Handoff

If you are the quarterback, the handoff is your responsibility. The runner has to worry about where he is going. *You* worry about getting him the ball.

As soon as you get the ball from the center, pull it right back into your stomach. Then when you get to the exchange point, put the ball firmly but smoothly in the runner's "pocket."

Keep two things in mind. First, look that ball right into his stomach. Stare right at his jersey, and hit the spot you aim at exactly. Burning your eyes right into his stomach is how you avoid a bad handoff—and a fumble. Second, lay the ball in gently. Some young quarterbacks think they need to slam the ball into the runner's stomach. But that just makes him flinch. It makes him think about the ball instead of where he's going. Just lay the ball in for him gently, like it's an egg. Let him get it without thinking about it.

If you are the runner, just before you reach the exchange point, make a good pocket to receive the ball. When the ball hits you, you'll close on it naturally—so don't *grab* for the ball. If you grab at it, you may knock it loose from the quarterback's hand. Take it easy. Just let him *give* you the ball.

Look that ball right into his stomach. Stare right at his jersey, and hit the spot you aim at exactly.

A second pocket variation: inside arm is still up high and horizontal, but outside arm is under the ball.

A third style: two hands under. Personally, I don't like this; the runner tends to grab at the ball.

89

The Pitchout

Just swing your arms and pitch it out there like a loaf of bread. They call it a dead-ball pitchout. The ball should just kind of hang in the air for easy picking.

The pitchout looks like one of the simplest things in football—but somehow it gives many young quarterbacks at our football camp a lot of trouble. Here are some tips we've developed over time:

The Pivot: Your coach will tell you whether to use a full pivot (a three-quarter pivot) or just a one-quarter or one-third pivot (what some quarterbacks call *opening out*).

Get Ready: If this were a handoff, you would first pull the ball back into your stomach. But you don't do that on a pass or a draw play, and you don't do it on a pitchout either. If you pull the ball back into your stomach, you can't pitch it—even though many young quarterbacks try to do it anyway. They kind of shove the ball in a weak way, and it doesn't have any zip. The ball carrier has to wait on it, and that's not good. We want to pitch that ball out in front of the running back so he can take it in stride—just as though we were throwing a pass. So here's what you should do. As you pivot, take the ball back beside your thigh pad, right alongside your leg (don't drop it any lower or you might throw the ball upward over the runner; a fairly horizontal pitch gives you less room for error).

The Pitch: Now zero your eyes in on the target, step straight in the direction you are pitching, and simply swing your arms. The eyes are vital; pick out a very specific target, not just the whole body of the runner. You'll be more accurate. I used to zoom in on his numbers and aim to pitch about a foot in front of those. As for the arm swing, be sure to keep your arms and elbows out away from your body, so the swing is free and easy. Then just toss the ball out there like a loaf of bread. My runners always told me it's easier to catch a pitch if it isn't spinning hard. It's called a dead-ball pitchout. Just pitch it out so it kind of hangs in front of the runner for easy picking.

To pitch out, first pivot and step straight where you want to throw the ball. As you turn, move the ball down beside your leg, right next to your thigh pad (don't pull the ball into your stomach first). Then just swing your arms and toss the ball out with no spin on it.

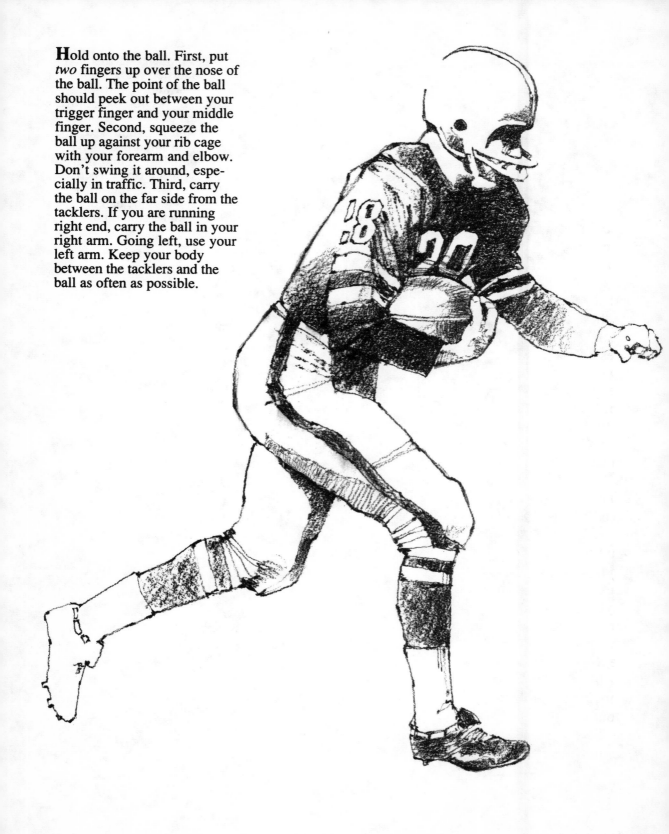

Hold onto the ball. First, put *two* fingers up over the nose of the ball. The point of the ball should peek out between your trigger finger and your middle finger. Second, squeeze the ball up against your rib cage with your forearm and elbow. Don't swing it around, especially in traffic. Third, carry the ball on the far side from the tacklers. If you are running right end, carry the ball in your right arm. Going left, use your left arm. Keep your body between the tacklers and the ball as often as possible.

The Runner

L et me tell you about one of the best efforts by a running back I ever saw. I was shocked. I was amazed. This was against the Raiders back in about 1967. We were behind by eight points with a minute or so left, and we hit a couple of passes out to our 48-yard line. I thought I'd run a draw play to Emerson Boozer, maybe get a few yards and slow down their rushers. So I give it to Boozer, he gets out there about ten yards, and they nail him. I'm chasing him to call another play right away, but just as I close on him, Boo takes off again. I chase him again, he's trapped again, I slow down—and there he goes. He went those whole 52 yards. They hit him seven times. He did two 360° turns. I don't ever hope to see a run any better than that one. Besides that, we got the two-point conversion and ended up with a tie.

So running backs can make a big contribution, and it's fun carrying the ball—if you get the blocking. But carrying the ball is a big responsibility, too. You shouldn't drop it. What a big thing this is. Don't fumble. The whole team moves the ball down the field. If you drop it, you feel terrible.

Kids sometimes pick up bad habits watching the pros. Maybe you see Walter Payton waving the ball around in one hand. But what you should understand is that Walter Payton is a great athlete with powerful hands. He can do things that maybe you shouldn't try yet. For tips on how to keep from fumbling, see the opposite page.

Mental Checklist: The other important thing for a runner is just like for everybody else. Have a mental checklist before every play. Use your head. On a running play you might have a four-point list. As you come out of the huddle, first repeat the snap count. Second, imagine clearly in your mind where the quarterback is going to give you the ball (the exchange point). Third, visualize exactly where you are supposed to run. Finally, repeat the snap count. Now you're ready.

> Don't fumble. Everybody has been working hard, moving the ball down the field—and then you *drop* it. It's an awful feeling.

Going into the line, you need a good forward lean. This keeps you down low, where you are harder to hit, and all it shows a tackler are your helmet, shoulder pads and knees. A good lean also gives you a lot of forward drive.

Runner's Lean

You watch most good runners going through the line and you'll see them charging down good and low—with their weight out front. Coaches call it the "runner's lean." It's a good hitting position, with an extra tip.

"You need a good lean going through the line," says Wade Wilson of the New Orleans Saints. "If you stand up going through there, they are going to drill you good."

Staying low also gives you the advantage on leverage. As San Francisco All-Pro Wendell Tyler says, "Heading into a collision, the runner should stay low. Most times, the man in the lower position wins."

When you run like that, all a tackler sees is your helmet and your shoulder pads and your knees. That's why you run down low with a good high knee action. You don't give the tackler anything good to hit.

"Running in traffic, you can bounce off a lot of people," says William Andrews, a great inside runner for the Atlanta Falcons for many years. "You just stay down and kind of balled up, with your shoulders down and your knees high, and you bounce off people like a rubber ball."

To do this right, you have to get a fast start. You need a good stance and a fast start to hit the line while the hole is still there. "You should be at three-quarters speed as you leave your stance," Andrews says, "and at top speed by your third step. It's like spraying gas into your carburetor."

One more thing helps you through the line: the right attitude. Get it in your mind that no one man can bring you down. You don't usually try to run straight over anybody (see page 100), and when people hit you from the side, just plow right through them. Attack their front arm and shoulder and refuse to go down. A lot of kids go down because somewhere inside they think, "Well, that's it. I'm tackled." No way. Give it a second effort. Give it a *third* effort. Explode on people and keep fighting them.

Coaches call it the "runner's lean." Runners stay down in a good hitting position, but leaning way forward.

Jim Taylor, Hall of Fame fullback, drives through the front arm of a tackler with high knees and a good runner's lean.

Follow Your Blockers

Sometimes a young runner just charges off on his own. You get that ball in your hands, and you just can't wait to get moving. You zoom off, leave all your blockers behind—and get creamed.

Here's a good thing to remember when you're running the ball. You don't have to do it all by yourself. In fact, you *can't* do it all by yourself. Your buddies are blocking for you. Let them help you.

Sometimes a young runner just charges off on his own. You get that ball in your hands, and you just can't wait to get moving. You zoom off, leave all your blockers behind—and get creamed.

Even the best pros have to relearn this lesson. Roger Craig of the San Francisco 49ers is one of the best backs in football, but when he first came into the NFL, he was in too big a hurry. "I had to learn to be patient," Roger says. "I had to learn to wait on my blockers and let them work for me. You can't do it by yourself."

This is why a runner should study up on his plays. Know who is blocking for you. Know where they are going to come from. Know who they are trying to block.

"I used to imagine a game while I was running down the street back home," says my buddy, O.J. Simpson. "I'd imagine the tacklers, I'd imagine my blockers. Then I'd fake and cut. You need to have it all in your mind."

When you are running wide, stay tucked in right behind the blocker who is leading you.

Wait as long as you can, until your blocker makes his move and you can see your opening.

Make a sharp cut, and head upfield just as the block is being made— not after the tackler recovers.

Stick with your buddies as long as you can. They're trying to do a lot of the work for you.

Picking The Hole

Every time a play is called, trust the hole first. Trust the design of the play. Trust your teammates.

To make any yards, you've got to find a hole. You can't make many yards running through solid bodies. The first place to look for the hole is right where it's supposed to be. If your coach gives you a play between guard and tackle, then try like mad to *run* between guard and tackle.

A lot of young runners give up on the hole too quickly. Maybe the last time this play was called, it didn't work. So this time the runner gives up on the play before it even starts. That's no good. There are a lot of reasons why a play might not work once. Maybe a linebacker blitzed right into the hole. Maybe a blocker slipped. So every time a play is called, trust the hole first. Trust the design of the play. Trust your teammates. Then if you get the handoff and get up there and the hole doesn't open—*that's* when you start looking for daylight. (This works a little differently if your coach uses *option blocking*; see the pictures below).

What this also means is, stay with the play until you get the handoff. You don't have to *look* for the handoff. You look at the hole, and let the quarterback take care of the handoff. But you do have to run right where you are supposed to until you get the ball—even if the hole is stuffed.

Option blocking means your blocker has an option whether to block his man to the right or left.

If your coach gives you an option blocking play, then watch the key blocker carefully.

If you see the defensive color on the right of your blocker, then make a full-speed cut to your left.

If you know where
your blockers are
supposed to come
from, and who they
are supposed to hit,
it's easy for you to
cut into the hole.

Don't run right at a guy, but don't run all the way around him either. You want to fake just enough—and cut just enough—to get the tackler off-balance. Then run through his arm. The closer you stay to this tackler, the farther you remain from all the others.

Faking Them Tight

You don't want to hit many tacklers head on. Even if you are a lot bigger than the other guy, a head-on collision is the slowest way to go. The tackler may go down, but you get slowed up, too. You may even trip over the fallen body.

On the other hand, you can't run all the way around many people either. "You can't take the great circle route very often," says O.J. Simpson, who ran his way into the Hall of Fame. "By the time you run all the way around one guy, three other guys catch up to you."

So the best way, in O.J.'s words, is to "fake them tight." Fake the tackler just a bit, then cut close him, even if he gets an arm on you. Run hard and just run through his arm. This is the way to get upfield fastest.

Mike Pruitt has been an All-Pro, and he agrees with Simpson. "There's no way I want a tackler to get a straight shot on me," he says. "What I do is give the guy a little move, a hip or head fake, then cut just enough to hit him in a weak spot. If you can juke him just enough, then run through one of his arms instead of hitting him head on, you should be able to defeat his tackle."

If you do get trapped, however, and there's no way out, it's best to dip way down into a good hitting position—and pop right out at the guy. *You* deliver the blow. Don't just take it. At least that's the opinion of Walter Payton, the great halfback on the Chicago Bears—and many other runners as well. Says Wilbert Montgomery, "If you hit the guy harder than he hits you, he'll be worried the next time he has a shot at you. Get a good lean. Keep your head up so you don't just plow into the dirt. Then explode into the tackler. Even when they've got you cold, you can get two or three more yards."

The best way, in O.J.'s words, is to "fake them tight." Fake the tackler just a bit, then cut close to him, even if he gets an arm on you.

The Stiff-Arm

You don't have to knock the guy flat. All you have to do is hit him in the right spot at the right time.

One of the great all-time weapons for the runner is the stiff-arm. It can do great things for you. Here comes some big guy running up ready to tackle you—and Pow! you hit him with a stiff-arm and you're gone.

The thing is, you don't have to knock the guy flat. All you have to do is hit him in the right spot at the right time. Just give him a shot, he can't make his grab, and you slip on past.

The first thing about a stiff arm is where to aim it. That depends on how he's coming at you. If you are running away from him toward the sideline, and he's standing up as he reaches for you, sometimes you can hit him a good shot to the chest or the closest shoulder. But if he's down in a good position, go for his helmet—the forehead or the top of his head. That will be the closest target. *Don't* aim at his mask. You can get a finger tangled up and cause yourself grief.

The other thing is, don't stick your arm out for a long time. If you leave it out there long, he'll use it as a handle and pull you down. What you want to do is wait until the last second. Just when he thinks he's home free, he's got you, that's when you shoot it out. Like a jab in boxing. Just jolt him and take off.

Don't put your arm out too soon. If you put it out and leave it, the tackler is just going to grab onto it and pull you down.

102

The Blockers

The linemen are the heart of the running game. It's not an easy job. A good offensive blocker has to be strong and aggressive—but you can't be *too* aggressive. It has to be a *controlled* aggression.

The quarterback can handle the ball perfectly. The runner can have all his techniques down cold. But let me tell you something. If the line doesn't block, we're all going nowhere. Blocking is the basis of the running game.

We can always help the blockers, of course. If we call good plays, mix things up and keep the defense off-balance, we can make it easier on the blockers. Hey, if the defense knows ahead of time that we're going off tackle, that makes it awfully tough. So you mix up the plays.

Sometimes one guy on your line will just be overmatched. No matter how good you are, you'll run into somebody better—somewhere, sometime. I remember back at Alabama we had a fine center. Great blocker. But this one day he was up against a nose tackle who later wound up in the pros. And he just couldn't handle him. He came back to the huddle screaming, "I just can't *block* that guy." It happens. So you give him some help. You double team that guy, or trap him sometimes. Give your blocker some help.

But basically, the linemen have to take care of business. They are the heart of the running game. It's not an easy job. A good offensive blocker has to be strong and aggressive—but you can't be *too* aggressive. We've talked about this already. You can't get down in your stance and say, "Now I'm going to *nail* this guy." Then you fire out at him with all your might—and he moves. He goes left or right. Or backs up. You crash to the ground, and he nails your *runner*.

So an offensive lineman needs to be aggressive. But it has to be a *controlled* aggression. It takes a great deal of discipline. You have to keep your wits about you, use the right techniques, keep yourself under control.

When you get blockers like that, it makes the game easier. I can tell you from personal experience. If the line gets whipped, we all get whipped. But if the line has things under control, then the game is a lot of fun.

Pulling Out

Another basic move of the lineman is to pull out. You do that to trap, or cross block, or lead a sweep or a quick screen.

We already covered the most basic block in football—the shoulder block. That was back in the section called The Basics, on page 66. Every offensive lineman should study that section thoroughly and practice that block until it's second nature. Work on a blocking dummy. Work against your buddies. Get all those techniques down cold. You can't be a blocker at all if you can't throw the shoulder block.

Another basic move of the lineman is to pull out—to step out sideways instead of straight ahead, and run laterally behind the line of scrimmage. You do that to throw a trap block or a cross block, or to lead a sweep or a quick screen pass. It used to be that only the guards did much pulling.

The centers and tackles usually blocked straight ahead. But in modern football, coaches want all the linemen to pull at times. Even at center or tackle, if you can pull out well, you'll have a better chance to play.

If you want to pull out of there quickly, first you have to have the right stance. Review what we said on page 60. You have to be well-balanced. You can't have too much weight forward on your hand. If your weight is forward, you have to regroup yourself before you can start moving sideways. That takes too much time. So get in a good, well-balanced stance to begin with—with your feet spread comfortably, your weight on the balls of your feet, and not too much weight forward on you hand. A good stance makes for a good start.

Pivot on the left toe, turn the right foot—*and* whip the right arm back so hard that it turns your whole upper body to the right.

To pull well, work on these moves at every practice (reverse the words *right* and *left* to pull left):

First Stage: Set your feet as you do for your stance. Put your elbows on your knees. Now do two things at once. Pivot on the ball of your left foot—and place your right foot at a 90° angle (see diagram). Don't take a big step with the right foot. Practice until you can do both moves in one motion.

Second Stage: Now pivot on the left foot, turn the right foot —*and* whip the right arm back so hard that it turns your whole upper body to the right. That right arm whip is really important. Pull yourself around—but stay down low.

Third Stage: Do the pivot-step-whip as one move—and sprint away to the right. Run straight down the line—don't swerve back into your backfield. Run with a runner's lean.

When you feel good doing this from the "up" position, practice all the same moves from the three-point stance. Then reverse *right* and *left* and practice pulling to the left.

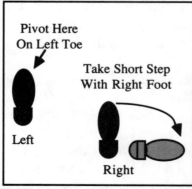

Pulling 90° right: pivot on ball of left foot and place right foot at 90° to right. Take only a small step.

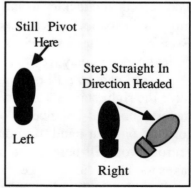

Pulling 45° right (on trap or cross block): Point first step exactly where you are headed.

While you are pulling, you want to stay down low in a good hitting position. It speeds you up, and it keeps you ready to block anyone who might pop up at any second.

The Trap Block

Here comes a defensive lineman charging really hard into your backfield. He's got his ears back, smoke is coming out of his helmet. Now you trap him.

I think the trap block must be the most fun to throw for any lineman. A lot of times you get to catch the guy from his blind side and really pop him. Of course, other times he sees you coming. Then you better have your helmet strapped on tight.

You trap a defensive lineman who is charging really hard into your backfield. He's got his ears back, smoke is coming out of his helmet. Maybe he's blown in there and torn a play apart. Now you trap him. One of your buddies down the line just lets the guy charge in. Gets out of his way. The guy is charging across the line, ready to eat some runner for lunch, and Wham! you pull out and blast him from the side.

To do a trap, just keep a few points in mind. First, pull out as you learned already. Run down low, down in a good hitting position. That means you have good balance and can move the way you need to hit the guy. Also, take your first step in the direction where he lined up. Coaches say, "Go down into the hole after him." This is in case he *doesn't* charge. You start right at him and if he decides to stay at home, you can still hit him. If he *is* charging, you just swerve a little bit and catch him in the side.

The left guard traps the right tackle's man. Notice that the left guard starts down into the hole, right where the defensive end lined up. Then, if the end charges, you swerve slightly to hit him.

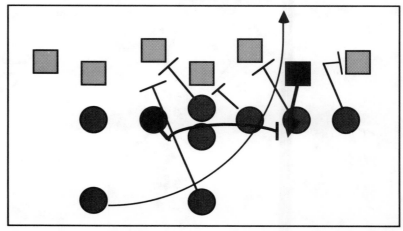

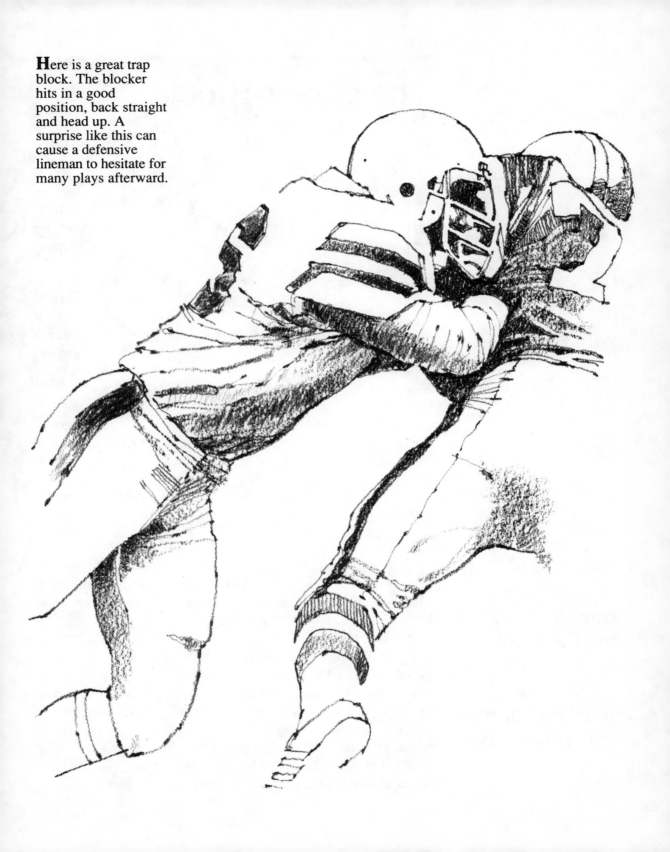

Here is a great trap block. The blocker hits in a good position, back straight and head up. A surprise like this can cause a defensive lineman to hesitate for many plays afterward.

The Cross-Block

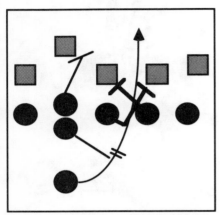

Here the outside blocker goes first. Inside blocker takes one "pull step," (toe aimed 45° to the right) then crosses.

The cross-block is like a close trap. You and the lineman next to you exchange targets. He blocks your man and you get his.

Here's another block you pull to make. The cross-block is like a trap, but it's a close trap. Really, just you and the lineman next to you exchange targets. He blocks your man and you get his.

Usually the outside blocker goes first—but your coach will tell you what he wants on each play. Say you are the right guard and your buddy at right tackle goes first. He executes a *down block*—a block on the first man to his inside. He fires on an angle into the man, getting a good shoulder block with his right shoulder—and his head in front of the guy. Meanwhile, you take a first pull step and aim your foot right at your target. Let your tackle go by, then slant down right behind him and kick his man out with a right shoulder block.

If you execute the cross block right, a big hole opens for the runner. The key is for the first blocker to fire fast and for the second blocker to take that pull step to let the first man go by.

This pulling guard is in
good hitting position.
Don't start your block
too soon, or you'll get off-
balance and miss. Vince
Lombardi used to say,
"Wait until you're
stepping on their toes."

Downfield Blocking

You may think that a lineman doesn't really need much speed. Well, downfield blocking will prove you wrong. Going downfield you have to stay in front of your runner—and you have to catch up to those little defensive backs. It takes some speed, first of all. So even the big guys should work hard on those speed techniques.

Blockers usually like downfield blocking. In the first place, one good downfield block can mean a touchdown. Gene Upshaw was one of the great All-Pro guards (now he is head of the player's union). Upshaw used to love to pull out and lead the runner around end. "That was my main play," Upshaw says. "That's where it comes down to just you and the defensive back. If you get him clean, you're going to make a long gain. If you miss him, you won't get a yard."

You pull out low and hard, legs driving and toes pushing off. Stay way down in a good hitting position, which is also a good sprinting position. "The thing to think about most is getting out of your stance right on the count and going full speed," says Upshaw. "You and your runner really have to move. There is nothing but trouble chasing you."

Stay down in that good hitting position and look for your man. Your coach will tell you which guy to look for—probably the cornerman or the safety. But regardless, be sure to plow over the first guy you see. Don't pass anybody up.

To make the block, aim right for his chest. Go right for the middle of him. Then, at the last minute, hit with the best shoulder. He may move, but if you go right for his chest at first, you'll be able to move with him and get him.

"Just have it in your head that whatever the guy does, it has to be wrong," says Upshaw. "If he goes out, put him out of bounds. If he goes in, turn him in. And if he stands there, man, go right over the top of him."

Remember, *you can't spear* with your helmet, and blocking downfield, you can't go low at his legs.

> Stay down in that good hitting position and look for your man. Your coach will tell you which guy to look for. But mostly you're going to plow over the first guy you see.

Backs As Blockers

Every now and then we see a young runner who has a big head. He'll think he's so good carrying the ball that he doesn't have to block. All that means is he won't play very long.

Every young player should practice every phase of the game. A runner, for instance, should practice his catching—and his throwing, too. Be a good, well-rounded player, and your team can make good use of you. That means you'll play more. And enjoy it more.

For running backs, one thing this means for sure is that you've got to be able to block. If you can block, when you're not carrying the ball you can still help your team. Everybody will notice, believe me. If you throw a good block, your teammates are going to love you. If you hide out or get lazy, they'll be really upset.

Every now and then we see a young runner who has a big head, a cocky attitude. He'll think he's so good carrying the ball that he doesn't have to block. All that means is he won't play very long. Heck, even quarterbacks have to block in some systems. Back at Alabama, we had a halfback who led the nation in scoring. His name was Cotton Clark, and our favorite play on the goal line was a pitchout to Cotton. I had to block on the play, and sometimes I did it right. It felt good to be part of a touchdown that way.

To be a good blocker, all you need are two things: desire and technique. First, you have to want it. Second, you have to know what you're doing.

As you head in to block your man, do it like a lineman on an openfield block—but be even lower. Head towards your man in a good hitting position. You're probably smaller than the man you're blocking, so you definitely have to get underneath his pads (in most cases, however, you must hit him above the waist; hitting in the legs is illegal unless your man is in the middle of the line). Aim your head right for his midsection. Then at the last second, switch to a shoulder block with whichever shoulder makes most sense (remember, it's illegal to hit with your head). Keep your head up, hit upwards, and keep your feet shoulder width and driving.

A good block by
the lead back is
often the key to a
first down or a
touchdown. If you
do it well, you'll
be a popular guy
on your team.

PART THREE

Stopping The Run

Stopping The Run

We've talked about how to run the ball. Now it's time to flip the coin. It's time to talk about *stopping* the run. Offense gets a lot of glory—but defense wins a lot of games. And stopping the run is the basis of defense.

Think about it. If you can't stop the other team from running the ball, how are you going to win? They just cruise up and down the field. They never have to do anything risky. If I'm the quarterback and you center me the ball and all I have to do is run straight ahead—we win!

Running the ball is also the safest thing for the offense. The worst that can happen is a fumble—and if the runner is careful, he won't fumble much. But passing—first off, there are so many ways to throw an interception. Maybe the quarterback throws a bad pass. Maybe the receiver slips and falls down. Maybe the quarterback or the receiver doesn't read the defense right. Maybe a defensive back makes a good play. Maybe a defensive lineman bats the pass. Throwing the ball is simply more risky than running. Plus, standing there in the pocket, the quarterback is in a bad position if he's hit from the blind side. How many times have you seen the quarterback get hit in the back and cough up the ball?

So the defense has to *force* the offense to throw the ball. You have to stop the run. And the key to doing this—the key to all defense—is to play as a team. Each guy on the defense has his own job. If you do *your* job, and if all the other guys do *their* jobs, then the team will succeed. Too many kids see the ball get snapped and they just *chase* the ball—or what they *think* is the ball—and they forget what they are supposed to do. But defense can't work like that. It can't be helter-skelter. Everybody has to stay home first, take care of his own business—*then* go get the ball. I do my job. You do your job. You can count on me. I can count on you. That's team defense. That's how to stop the running game. And that's how to win.

121

The linemen are the front line of defense. They are first to engage the offense.

The Line

To stop the running game, you start with the front line. We call them the "down linemen" because they line up with one or both hands down on the ground. These are the guys that have to tear up the running offense.

These front guys don't always get to be heroes. The *linebackers* get to be heroes. They make more of the tackles, and get to hear their name called out by the announcer. But it's the down linemen that make it all possible. If you're down there in the pit, you have to do the job for your teammates. You often have to attack the other team's blockers, stop them in their tracks, knock them back, tie them up. That leaves your linebackers free to move.

I don't mean you just hit a blocker and give up. After you've stopped your man, then you play football, too. You find the ball and get to it. You'll get your tackles. But the first thing is to beat the offense on the line.

The worst thing that can happen to a defensive lineman is to get knocked backwards. We never want that to happen. If you get knocked back, first you're giving up yards. Second, you're getting in your linebackers' way. They can't move sideways to get in front of the play.

So you have to start off down in a good stance (see page 60). You may have a little more weight forward than an offensive lineman because you have to explode forward and keep from being driven back. Also, you might want to try this: turn your toes in a little pidgeon-toed in your stance. It will give you more power. (Want to prove this to yourself? Put your hands up against a wall and lean into it at a 45° angle. First turn your toes outward and push against the wall. Then turn your toes inward and push. Feel the difference? There is something about the pidgeon-toed position that lets your muscles work more efficiently. You get more drive.)

Exactly how you play your position will depend on your coach, but the following basic techniques will always help.

If you're down there in the pit, you have to do the job for your teammates. You often have to attack the other team's blockers, stop them in their tracks.

123

The goal of the *jam:* drive your man straight up, extend your arms, get a good grip on his jersey or shoulder pads. Linebackers also want to do this, to drive the blocker up in the air where you can control him. Don't ever let him get his shoulder into your body. Keep him away from you.

Attack Your Man

The way most defenses work, the first thing you have to do on every play is: whip your man. If he whips you —if he knocks you back off the ball—you've lost the battle. If you whip him, the offense is in trouble.

The secrets are (1) a good stance, (2) a hard charge and (3) leverage. You have to get underneath that blocker and knock him back on his heels. There are two ways to do this. One is with your shoulder—hit your shoulder under his pads and flip up your forearm to knock him upward (review this technique on page 64). The other is the *jam*, as you see here. Use your hands. Hit him under the shoulder pads and straighten your arms all the way out. You need strength for this, but mostly it's a question of angles, of technique.

If he whips you—if he knocks you back off the ball —you've lost the battle. If you whip him, the offense is in trouble.

The jam: drive straight at your man with your back flat and your head up. Put your hands in pushup position and bang the guy hard just *under* his shoulder pads. Don't hit straight into him; his force might knock you back. Hit *under* his pads, and hit *upwards*. Then his momentum towards you will be diverted upwards.

DAVE BOSS

125

Shedding Your Man

Beating the blocker is not enough, however. Once you have control of that man, you have to get rid of him. You want to go to the ball.

Getting that first good hit on your blocker is called the "jam" or the "sting." You really have to pop him. Many defensive linemen do this from the lower four-point stance (see page 60). "I line up down in almost a three-quarter squat, where I can get a lot of spring in my legs," says All-Pro nose tackle Fred Smerlas of the Buffalo Bills. "And I keep my back arched so my head is up. If I get what I call a 'turtle back,' all bowed up, I lose my whole sting. When the ball is snapped it's just one rocking motion—the hips, shoulders and arms all going up to stun him under the shoulder pads and knock him up in the air."

Beating the blocker is not enough, however. You can get a good jam, get leverage on your man—and then watch while the runner goes right by you. That's no good. Once you have control of that blocker, you have to get rid of him.

"We call this the *shed*," says Rubin Carter, long a star defensive lineman for the Denver Broncos. "The key is whether you had a good jam in the first place. If you jammed your blocker and got good extension in your arms and stood him up, then you can shed him. Throw him one way, clogging up that side, and then the runner has to come to you."

As you finish the *jam*, you should have a good, firm grip on his jersey or on his shoulder pad.

When you see where the play is going, use your grip to shed the man, to throw him away.

The *shed* not only gets rid of the blocker. It gives you momentum to go chase the ball carrier.

Many young defensive linemen forget they have to find the football. Hit your man a good pop, but then, Bing! cut your eyes to look for the ball. You have to play ping pong with your eyes—first your blocker, then the ball, then your blocker, and so on. Number 74 here has already seen where the play is going and started to shed his man.

When you shoot the gap, stay down low and come through in a good hitting position, with back straight and head up.

Shooting The Gap

Sometimes your coach won't want you to drive right into the man in front of you. Instead he'll want you to *shoot the gap*, slant off to one side of the blocker or the other. The idea is to penetrate. Get into the offensive backfield and cause some trouble.

To do this right, first *stay low*. If you lift up as you try to go by your blocker, he's going to knock you into the next county. You'll need bus fare to get back to the field.

Second, try to get by without hitting your man—but if you have to, pop him a good shot with your forearm. Say you want to go to your left. Take your first driving step with you *right* foot—on an angle across in front of the guy. At the same time, load up and be ready to pop him under his pads with your right forearm in case he comes at you.

Third, as you start to take your second step, wind up with your left forearm in case the guy next to you tries to block you. If he comes at you, pop him, too.

Finally, come through the gap with your shoulders square to the line of scrimmage and your head up. Don't be turned at an angle. Square up with your eyes open, so you can make a tackle right now—or go either way immediately.

When you shoot the gap, you slant off to one side of the blocker or the other. The idea is to get into the offensive back-field and cause some trouble.

In a gap defense, all the defensive linemen and linebackers take a particular *gap*—an area between two offensive blockers. Either you just *go* to your gap (big arrows), or you go on to *shoot* the gap (small arrows). Either way, a gap defense is sometimes easier for smaller linemen, because they don't have to hit head-on into the blocker in front of them.

Reading Your Man

If the guy across from you doesn't try to block you, you can bet someone else is coming after you.

Playing defensive line, you have to use your head. Sometimes you have to *read* the man in front of you. It's true you can't always see where the ball is going on your first step; the offensive backfield may run a couple fakes. But you *can* see where your *blocker* is headed. And where he goes is usually where the play winds up.

Here are a few simple tips for *reading*. Your coach may give additional instructions. Reading is simple to practice. You can do it by yourself. Get down in your stance and imagine the moves of your blocker. Then you react. You can also get a buddy and practice together—full-speed if you have equipment, or else just go through the motions.

1. Straight Ahead: If the blocker comes right at you, fight him. Most likely the ball is coming somewhere nearby.

2. Pulls Inside: If your blocker steps to your inside, the play is probably inside. *Stop your penetration.* Don't just crash across the line, or some other guy may trap you from the inside. So stop, slide down the line to the inside—and look out for a blocker from that side. If someone hits you, fight *through* the block. Drive right into the block. Don't try to run around it. As the coaches say, "Fight through pressure." If you try to run all the way around a block from the side, instead of fighting straight through it, it will take too long. The runner will be gone. So drive into that blocker, and at least try to push him back into the path of the runner.

3. Pulls Outside: If your blocker steps outside, the play is probably outside. Follow step 2, but toward the outside.

4. Drops Back: If your blocker drops back away from you, it's probably a pass. Rush the passer all out—unless your coach wants you to watch for a draw play or screen pass.

Basic Keys For Defensive Linemen

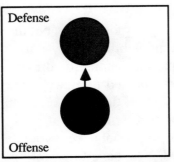

If the offensive lineman (black circle) comes directly at you, then your should read it as a running play. You are firing out at him anyway, so keep coming and play the run as hard as you can.

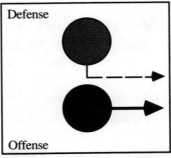

If the offensive lineman starts to his right, stop your penetration straight ahead, look into the backfield to find the ball, and shuffle down the line in the same direction (see page 141). If someone blocks you from that direction, fight straight through the block.

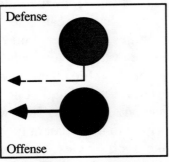

If the offensive lineman starts to his left, read run in that direction. Shuffle left and fight through any blocks on you from that side.

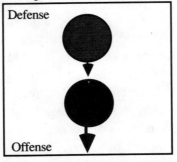

If the offensive lineman backs up to pass block, read pass. Keep coming straight ahead as hard as you can, but watch out for a draw play or screen pass.

One more tip: watch out for a *sucker* play. If your blocker pulls left or right, look into the backfield as you start to shuffle after him. The offense may be running a surprise play right at you.

The Linebackers

Linebackers have a lot of responsibility. That's why, if you want to play linebacker, your basic techniques have to be very good.

One of the linebackers is usually the defensive "quarterback." He's the guy who calls out defensive signals (like Number 51 at right) and tells his teammates what defense to run.

Helping lead the defense is a big responsibility, but then all the linebackers have a lot of responsibility. They must play against the running game, the passing game, the draw game and the screen game. They are expected to charge forward and make tackles in the offensive backfield as well as sprint backward and break up passes way downfield.

That's why, if you want to play linebacker, your basic techniques have to be very good. You have to patrol up and down the line of scrimmage—so you need to be able to move with agility. In most defenses you make the bulk of the tackles. That means you'd better be a good tackler. You'd better have excellent tackling technique (see page 68). Ideally, on any play, you want to get in front of the runner in a good hitting position and make the tackle square. Hit him a real shot and drive him backward. But it doesn't always work like that. You often have to make running tackles from the side or behind—and get people down any way that you can.

If you do work on your techniques, however, you *can* play linebacker well—even if you aren't the biggest or fastest kid in school. I think of guys on my Jets team, Larry Grantham and Paul Crane, who weren't very big, but played the game smart. They got a lot done on *awareness*. They were aware of the correct techniques—how to move laterally, how to play off blockers, how to make good tackles. They were aware of the types of plays each offense liked. They knew what to expect during a game. Plus, they were aware how to *read* the offense, how to look at one or two players on the offense and get a key on what play was coming. To play linebacker well, you need that awareness. You have to have your mind in the game.

When the play starts, linebackers have to watch the offense carefully, and *read* the play based on the first movements of the offensive players.

Reading The Play

Everybody on defense needs to be able to *read* a little bit—to look at the offense start its play and figure out what to do right away. But the linebackers especially have to cover a lot of ground. They have to defend against every type of play. They need to read well and get started fast.

Your first job is to recognize whether the offensive play is a run or pass. The simplest way to do this is to watch the offensive linemen. It's a simple fact of football life: if it's a run, they are trying to take ground away from you, so the linemen are going to fire out toward you. But if it's a pass, and you're a linebacker back off the line, it's *illegal* for them to come across the line and hit you. So they'll usually back up to pass block. In short: if they fire at you, play run. If they back up, play pass (but watch out for the draw or screen).

In addition to reading the linemen, you'll also probably key on a back. You read *through* the line and see the back as well. This sounds harder than it is. They are both right in front of you. Just don't get tunnel vision—don't focus on only one guy. Be aware of the linemen in front of you, and also pick up on the back who is your key. Your coach will tell you which back, depending on the type of defense you use.

The linebackers have to defend against every type of play. They need to read well and get started fast.

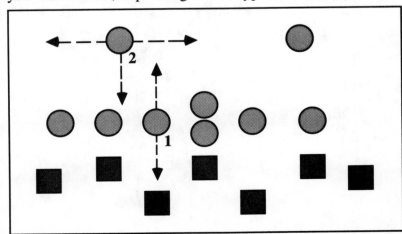

The left inside linebacker (black square) might key on the guard in front of him (1), and the closest back (2). Your coach will tell you exactly how he wants you to play—but, for instance, if the guard comes right at you, play run. If he drops back away from you, play pass. The motion of the back—left, right or straight ahead—can give you more information, depending on that team's offense.

The linebacker (left) keeps the blocker at arm's distance. You must master the jam and keep blockers away from you.

Playing Off The Blocker

A linebacker treats blockers as if they had the plague. You don't want them to get anywhere near you. Of course, sometimes you have to take them on with your shoulder—give them a real shot—but usually you try to keep your distance. You can't spend your time fussing around with that blocker. Pretend he's a hot stove. Get away from him as fast as possible—and go get the ball carrier.

The way to do this is: never let a blocker get his shoulder into you. Never let him into your body. If he gets his shoulder under your pads, he's going to shove you around—and it will be too late to make the play when you finally get free.

To prevent this, you have two choices. First, you can hit *him* before he hits *you*—pop him under the pads with your shoulder. Or, even better, jam him with your hands. "A linebacker has to use his hands," says Matt Blair, for many years an All-Pro with the Minnesota Vikings. "You give up your hands to save your body."

Every linebacker must master the *jam* (see page 124). One of the best all-time linebackers was Jack Ham of the Pittsburgh Steelers. He covers the basics of the jam this way: "You are lined up in a good hitting position to begin with—down low and ready to strike. When the blocker comes at you, you drive upward with your legs and deliver a blow with your hands to his chest, right under his shoulder pads. You try to stand him almost straight up—and get a good grip on the lower part of his pads, or his jersey. When you control him like that, you can shove off and make the tackle."

Once again it's a battle for leverage. All over the field, players fight these individual battles for control of their opponents. Leverage is one of the key techniques of football, and good techniques win games. As Ham says, "When you see a big play in the fourth quarter, more often than not you are seeing one guy who held his concentration and out-techniqued another guy in the clutch."

> You don't want to let blockers get into your body. You want to get away from them as fast as possible. Treat them like a hot stove.

Containment

Everybody has a job on defense. It's not like Grand Central Station—with people scurrying off in every direction. Everybody has a job. And everybody has to *do* his job, or the whole defense falls apart.

One of the key jobs is *containment*. Somebody on each side of the defense has to be the outside wall. He has to *contain* the play, turn it back in toward all his partners on the defense. They are chasing the runner in a controlled way (see next page) and they are counting on you to stop that runner from just sprinting away. If the contain man sluffs off, the ball carrier gets outside all by himself—loose down the sideline for the big gain or touchdown.

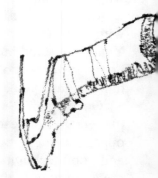

Sometimes the contain man is a defensive end, sometimes a linebacker, sometimes even a safetyman or cornerback. Your coach will tell you if you are the contain man—and *when*. Listen up. You don't want everybody mad at you because you let the runner escape to the outside.

When your job is containment, you don't necessarily have to make the tackle to do your job right. In fact, if you shoot in too hard to tackle the guy, he may juke right around you and get free outside. You have to play it smart. You have to take the correct angle on the play and make sure that if you miss him, at least he has to go inside.

Of course, you can't wait too far outside and just wave at the runner either. Says Donnie Shell, Pittsburgh's All-Pro safety, "A guy could stand clear out by the sidelines and say he was turning the play in. But then the runner has a hole thirty yards wide to run through."

After you practice awhile, you'll learn to gauge it right. Stay down in a good hitting position. Try to get across the line and force the runner to cut back sooner than he wants to. If a blocker comes at you, go attack him. Don't just stand there, or he'll run you over. And hit him with your *inside* shoulder, so your outside arm is still free if the runner tries to slip outside.

Here number 53 has *containment* responsibility. He has to force the runner to turn back to the inside. If you turn the runner back in, then your buddies can get him even if you miss the tackle.

The shuffle lets you move sideways behind the line without having to turn and run. You can see well, and you are always facing forward in case you need to take on a blocker or make the tackle.

The Shuffle

Linebackers don't run—until they *have* to. Whenever they can, they "shuffle." They scuttle sideways, like a crab, keeping their head and shoulders facing square into the offensive backfield.

Why should you do this? Can't you move faster if you just turn and run? Yes, of course. But speed is not always the number one thing. "If the ball carrier is moving sideways in the backfield," says Mike Singletary, the Chicago Bears All-Pro, "the biggest mistake you can make is to run all-out and catch up with him. If you get even with him, that's just what he wants. He cuts back behind you and goes straight upfield."

So what you do is shuffle down the line as long as you can (see pictures below). You keep your head and shoulders square to the line of scrimmage, so if the runner cuts back you can move with him. "If you keep your shoulders square," Singletary says, "then you are always in position to do business. And you can also protect your feet. If a blocker pops out at you low, you can get your hands on him, keep him off you, keep on going. If you turn your shoulders and start to run—start to really cross your legs over—a low blocker can pop out and chop you down like a big old tree."

Whenever they can, linebackers shuffle—they scuttle sideways like a crab, keeping their head and shoulders facing square into the offensive backfield.

All defensive linemen and linebackers should practice the shuffle a few minutes each day.

To shuffle left, step out with your left foot, close up with your right foot, then step out again.

Keep down in a good hitting position, with your shoulders square and your hands at the ready.

Chasing The Runner

You don't try to catch up to the runner—or he'll cut back behind you. You count on your containment on the outside, and stay slightly *inside*.

I f the play comes right at you as a linebacker, your job is obvious. You play off the blocker and put a real shot on the runner. Try to drive him straight back.

When you have to chase the play, however, things are more complicated. First, you try to shuffle sideways as long as you can—counting on your containment guy to turn the play back in to you. You don't have to sprint as long as your containment holds up. "My first couple of years," says Mike Singletary of the Bears, "I thought speed was everything. But I had so much to learn. You have to be patient. It takes time for plays to form. The idea is not just to be in the right place, but to be in the right place at the right time."

As you move sideways, you don't try to catch up to the runner—or he'll cut back behind you. You count on your containment on the outside, and *you* stay slightly *inside*. Even if your containment breaks down—maybe your guy gets knocked to the ground—you still chase the runner under control as long as you can. Keep your shoulders square to him, and stay slightly inside of him. Only in desperation—only if the runner is out there free and ready to turn upfield—do you just turn your shoulders and sprint.

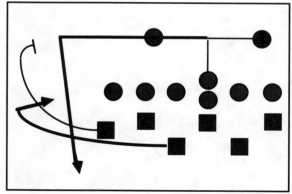

If you are playing inside linebacker (dark square), don't chase a runner so fast you overrun him and let him cut back inside you (through the *cutback lane*).

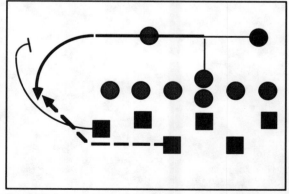

Instead, let your containment man *force* the play back inside. You chase under control, staying inside the runner, and *fill* the cutback lane from inside out.

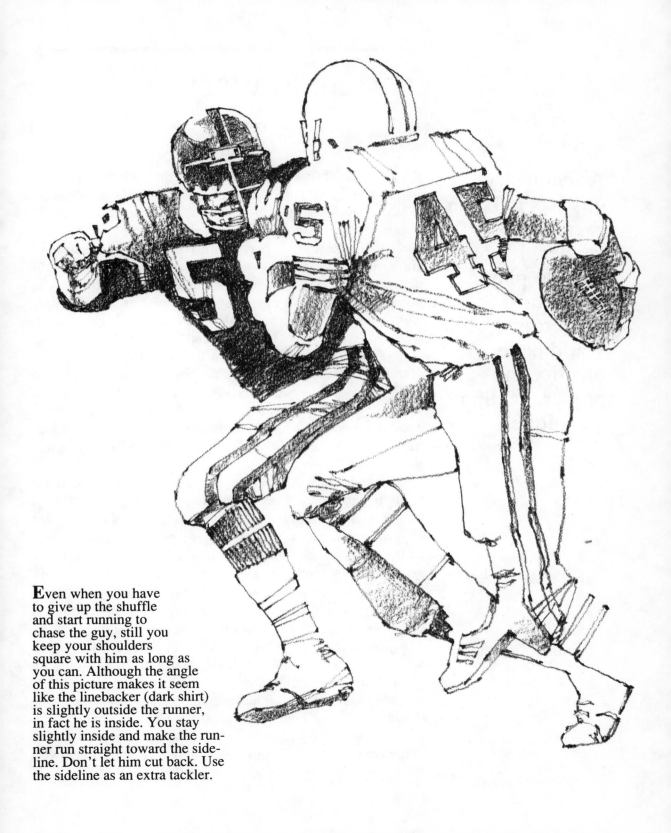

Even when you have to give up the shuffle and start running to chase the guy, still you keep your shoulders square with him as long as you can. Although the angle of this picture makes it seem like the linebacker (dark shirt) is slightly outside the runner, in fact he is inside. You stay slightly inside and make the runner run straight toward the sideline. Don't let him cut back. Use the sideline as an extra tackler.

The Secondary

A secondary guy has to be an excellent tackler. If you want to play safety or cornerman, you'd better practice the proper tackling techniques.

The defensive backs (the men in the *secondary*) are the last line of defense. If you are playing defensive back, and a runner gets by you clean, he'll probably score.

That's one reason a secondary guy has to be an excellent tackler. If you want to play defensive back, either safety or cornerman, you'd better practice the proper tackling techniques (page 72-77). I'll tell you another reason, too. You're going to run into a lot of running backs who are much bigger than you are. The coaches look for those great big fullbacks, so a smaller defensive back had really better know what he's doing. Be comfortable down in that hitting position, keep your head up and your eyes on his belt buckle, know how to strike a blow *underneath* his power—underneath his pads. If you just go charging in there any old way—if you come in standing up too high, or if you duck your head down and lose track of him—the runner will either run around you or power right through you.

A lot of coaches will tell you two things. First, if it's a really big guy, they'll say to hit him low—try to take his legs out from under him. On the other hand, if it's a little, quick guy, hit him *high*—it's easier to get a grab on him high, and he isn't big enough to knock you over. Both those points are good, but they won't always work. A lot of times you don't have any *choice* how you hit the guy. Maybe you're just getting rid of a blocker. Maybe the guy has made a good cut on you and you're not in position. In those kinds of cases, you just have to do what you can. Go high, go low, grab whatever you can—then *hold on*. Get a grip and slow him down until your buddies arrive.

One technique you should practice a lot is called *breaking down*. You may have to run top speed to get over to the runner, but then you usually want to break down—come under control and settle into a good hitting position. Otherwise the runner will cut, and you'll just go flying by.

144

A secondary man needs to be good at running fast, then *breaking down*. Here the safetyman has charged up to the line and now he's breaking down—slowing himself down and settling into a good hitting position, with legs spread, knees and waist bent into a crouch, and head up. Keep your weight on the balls of your feet, ready to move.

Run Support

One or two men in the secondary are usually assigned to *run support*. That means if the play is a run they have to come up fast and do a particular job to stop the run.

One or two men in the secondary are usually assigned to *run support*. That means if the play is a run they have to come up fast and do a particular job to stop the run. That doesn't mean that other guys in the secondary just loaf around if it's a run. But run support men have to be quicker and do their exact job—which is often containment.

The key is to figure out as fast as possible if it *is* a run. Just like linebackers, you read the play by watching the offensive linemen. It's usually easy to watch the guard and tackle on your side—and they'll tell you run or pass. If they go forward it's almost always a run; if they go back it's almost always a pass.

You have to read this as fast as possible. As a defensive back, your first responsibility is to play pass defense. You can't afford to get fooled by a fake run and then have a touchdown pass go over your head. But on the other hand, you can't stand back there until a running play is all over and then tell your coach you were playing for the pass. So read the movement of the line (don't watch the quarterback and the runners; they can fake a handoff easily to fool you) and get up to do your job as soon as you're sure.

Your coach will give you your keys in the defensive backfield. One possibility is shown here. The safety (dark square) keys on the tight end (1) and the closest guard (2). If the tight end blocks to his inside—and the guard is moving forward—then the safety shoots up to take his run support job (in this case, containment).

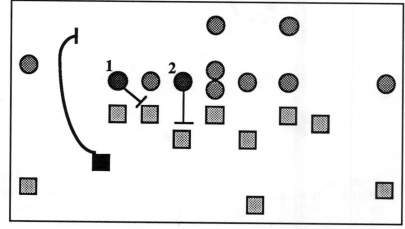

The safetyman has come up on run support to make the tackle. This is a good form tackle—back straight, head up, arms locked. Ideally, your head would be in *front* of the runner, but you can't always make a perfect tackle.

Hanging On

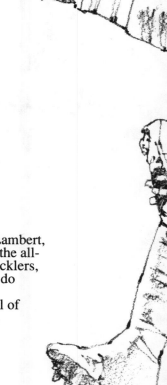

As a tackler in the defensive backfield, your number one job is clear: get a super-glue hold on that guy any way that you can. You are often the last man—the last hope your team has of stopping a touchdown. So go after each tackle with all-out desire.

It's good to have good tackling form, as we've already said. A good form tackle has the best chance of working—if you are in position to use it. But if you're not—if you're falling on your back or tripping over a blocker or making a desperation dive—then tackle the guy with sheer force of will power. Grab on to something—*anything*—and don't let go.

Maybe all you can get is one foot, or a handful of shirt. That's enough if you have great desire. You don't actually have to bring the guy down. Just clamp on like a bulldog and wait for your teammates to come help you out. With a big guy that may mean just jumping on his back and going for a ride. Give him a load to carry, and he'll slow down enough that your buddies can catch him.

As we said before, the secret to tackling is not just good form. It is "a burning desire to bring the runner down." Playing defensive backfield, that's certainly true.

Jack Lambert, one of the all-time tacklers, makes do with a handful of jersey.

BILL AMATUCCI

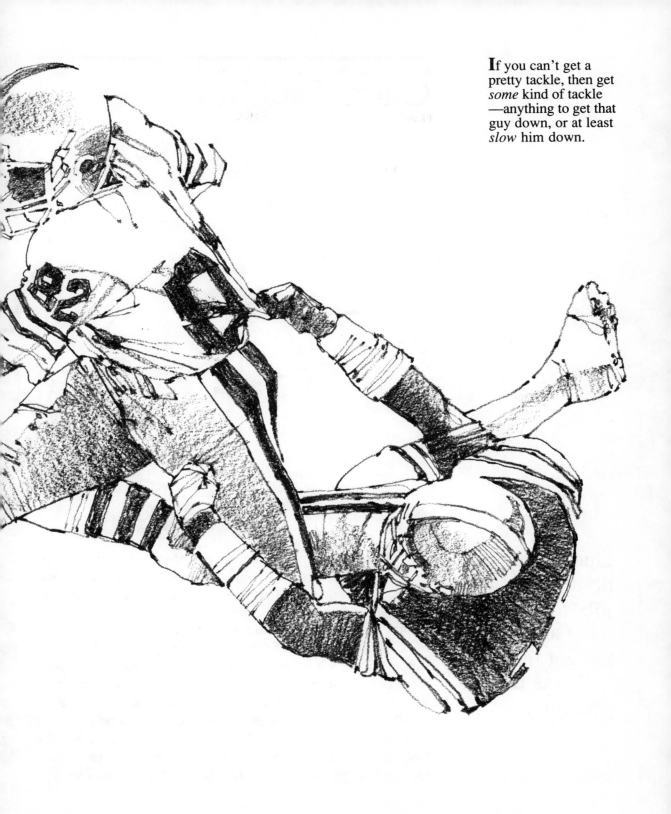

If you can't get a
pretty tackle, then get
some kind of tackle
—anything to get that
guy down, or at least
slow him down.

Gang Tackling

Once you have
done your first
job, then you
have a *new* one.
Go get the
ball—as fast as
possible.

150

You have to play as a team on defense. That means two things. First, do your own job. Do what the coach tells you to do first. If you are a lineman, maybe you are supposed to take one particular gap. If you are a linebacker, maybe you are supposed to key on one particular back. If you are a defensive back, maybe you have run support. Fine, whatever it is, you do that job first. Then your team can count on you. Everybody does his own job well, and the whole defense fits together like the fingers on a hand.

But there's something else. Once you have done your first job, your primary responsibility, then you have a *new* job. Once the play is under way, if the ball doesn't come to you, then *you* go get the *ball*—as fast as possible. In other words,

don't stand around and watch your teammates tackle the guy. Nobody on defense should be a spectator. First you check your responsibility. If the ball is going somewhere else, Boom! you're gone. You're running as hard as you can to get to the ball carrier and help out on the tackle.

There are a lot of reasons for this. In the first place, a good runner can beat any one tackler a lot of the time. Maybe your guy only gets an arm, or a leg. Or just makes the runner slow down. You've got to get there in time to help him out. Second, you always want to *gang tackle* a runner. As many guys hit him as possible. Over the course of a game, you can wear the runner out if he has to deal with three or four tacklers every time he touches the ball.

Pursuit Angles

The last thing you want is to get behind a guy and chase in his footsteps. So take an angle on the guy. Cut him off at the pass.

You want to run after the ball carrier and help gang tackle him. So where do you run? You just chase him, right? Nope. Not right. The last thing you want is to get behind a guy and chase in his footsteps. To chase a guy and catch him, you're going to need a motorcycle. He's got a head start. When you catch up to him, it will be too late.

So what you want to do is take an angle on the guy. Cut him off at the pass. We call this taking the correct *pursuit angle*. A lot of young defensive linemen and linebackers start off by charging into the offensive backfield. Then, if the play goes away from them, they just follow the runner from behind. No good. Take an *angle* on the guy.

How do you take the correct angle? First, your coach may tell you some things. He may want certain guys pursuing at certain angles. For sure he'll want *one* guy to stay back on the far side of the defense for a while and wait for a reverse or some other trick play. Beyond your coach's ideas, it's just practice. Just do it with your friends over and over. The runner can't go out of bounds. He has to turn up the field. So use that sideline as a twelfth man on defense. Let the sideline turn the guy in, and you take an angle to cut him off.

The farther you are away from the runner, the bigger the angle of pursuit you have to take. Practice chasing around the field with your friends until you get a good idea of the best angle to take in each different situation.

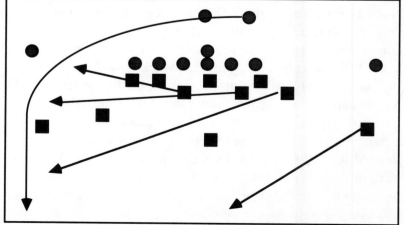

Keep your eyes open.
If you can hit the ball
while you make a good
tackle, then go ahead.
Otherwise, just go for
the tackle and let your
teammates come up
and go after the ball.

Stripping The Ball

Here's another good reason why everybody on defense wants to take a good pursuit angle and hustle as hard as possible. You not only want to stop the ball carrier as soon as possible. You also want to get the ball back for your team. The more guys we get to the ball, the more good things can happen for us.

If you watch pro football, you see a lot more defensive guys today trying to knock the ball loose from the ball carrier, or pull it loose. We call this *stripping the ball*. Obviously, it's one good thing if you tackle the guy, bring him down. But it's an even better thing if two or three of you can get in there and strip the ball loose. Why let them punt way downfield if you can get the ball right here?

The only problem with this is that you have to be careful. Very careful. You can't try to strip the ball and think so much about the ball that you miss the tackle. You get nothing, the guy runs by you for a touchdown, and you try to tell your teammates you were stripping the ball.

So my advice is this. If you're the first guy to the ball carrier, you *tackle* him. Don't worry about the ball. Worry about the guy. Get him stopped. Now if two or three of your buddies arrive, maybe one of them can dig after the ball. Gang tackling. That's what you want. The second or third guy can maybe strip that ball loose, and with more defensive players arriving all the time, there will be plenty of people around to fall on the ball.

That's just another way to know that team defense is the way to stop the running game. First, everybody does his own job. Hold up your own up end. Then, if the ball isn't right there in front of you, go find it. Take a good pursuit angle and run that ball carrier down. Help on a gang tackle. Maybe knock the ball loose, if somebody else has a good grip on the runner. Work with your buddies. It's a team game.

> If you're the first guy to the ball carrier, you *tackle* him. If two or three of your buddies arrive, maybe one of them can strip the ball and cause a fumble.

155

PART FOUR

The Passing Game

The Passing Game

Now it's time to talk about the passing game. It's fun to throw the ball out there, make some big plays, score some points. I know we've said the passing game is a bit riskier than running. And it is. But it's also fun, it's often necessary—and it's usually the fastest way to score points.

There's another good reason to pass. When you play offensive football, you want to have a balanced offense. You want to be able to run *and* pass. Then the defense has to play you honest; if they stop one, you go to the other. A balanced offense gives you more chances to win.

Go back to the year 1900. Back then passing the ball forward wasn't even legal. A football game was just 22 guys bunched right around the ball. The whole defense was right up there on the line. It was tough to make many yards when all you could do was run.

So in 1900 there were zero passes a game. Today there are maybe 60 or 70 in a typical pro game. Passing is a big part of football now. If you want to have a winning team, you have to be able to pass the ball. For that, you need two things. First, you need a line. That's right. The blockers. The best passer in the world can't do much flat on his back.

Second, you have to practice. The quarterback has to practice passing until he can throw the ball well enough. Then the quarterbacks and the receivers have to work together. A lot. If you want to be a passer or a receiver, you have to be the kind of guy who likes to practice. Me, I always loved it. It was fun throwing to my guys, trying to make each play perfect. We'd stay out after the team practice was over, and we'd work until we got things on the money.

It's easy if you love to play catch. And it's necessary. In the fourth quarter of some big game, with the rushers all around you and the whole game on the line, you and your receivers can do something great—if you got your moves and timing down cold in practice.

158

The quarterback has to deliver the ball accurately. To do this consistently, you should develop good passing form.

The Quarterback

To play quarterback, you should throw the ball well, and in order to throw well, you should have a good motion, good passing form. You should drill yourself on the basics over and over until the whole motion is automatic—until good form comes naturally, even in the last minute with the game on the line.

I'll tell you a story that shows this. This was in December, 1968. To get to the Super Bowl, we had to beat the Oakland Raiders for the AFC Championship. With four or five minutes to go, we were down 23-20, and we got the ball back deep in our territory. We needed yards quickly, and we got them. First, George Sauer caught a square-out, then Don Maynard ran deep past a cornerback playing bump-and-run and made a tremendous catch 60 yards out there, on about the Raider eight- or nine-yard line.

So now I'm running down the field thinking about what to call. And somehow I'm figuring, "They're going to look for a run." We had passed ourselves into good position, we had time for a run, and I just thought they'd be expecting it. Plus—and here's something from left field—Peter the cab driver had been telling me for a week or two how every time we got down close to the goal line, it seemed like we ran. I'd been listening to Peter the cab driver. So as I run down the field, I decide to fake a run and then pass. Great call. Peter will like it. But it doesn't work.

I fake to Matt Snell going left and look out to that side, but everybody on the Raiders is playing pass defense. My primary receiver is Sauer, but he's covered. My second receiver is Billy Mathis in the flat. Covered. My third guy is tight end Pete Lammons coming over the middle. *He's* covered. Now the rush is after me, and I'm down to my fourth receiver, Maynard. Only Don is back on the right side of the field. He's running a delayed crossing pattern. I'm trying to get myself back over to the right side so I can find him, but the field is

Any boy can learn to throw the ball well. Any boy who takes the time to learn the simplest, easiest way to throw the ball can throw it straight enough to win.

I'm going to show you a really simple way to throw. It's a style that takes very little arm action because it uses the natural power you can gain from turning your body.

really muddy and I slip. I take another step, and *that* foot slips. I'm trying to get my footing back and just then I see Maynard make his break.

Here's where the years of practice helped. With the footing that bad, with a bunch of guys after me, with me finding Maynard only at the last instant, still my body gathered itself and that pass went out with some *heat* on it. Matt Snell told me later he didn't see the ball but he heard it go by. Zip! Don caught it in the back of the end zone. Touchdown. We go to the Super Bowl. Believe me, at a time like that, all the practice you've done seems definitely worth it.

On that one pass, and throughout my career, I'm convinced that the throwing motion I worked on so long really made a difference. My brother Bob got me into it back on the streets of Beaver Falls, and I polished it with every pass I threw over the years—even just warming up. It's a simple, efficient motion that makes for a quick and powerful release, and I'm convinced it can help any young passer throw better.

Most quarterbacks you see take a big wind-up before they throw. They look like baseball pitchers, with a big, loose arm action. The ball goes up, down, around—and that's a problem. First off, if you wind up awhile in order to throw, you give all the defensive people time to react. They can close ground on your receiver while you're trying to get rid of the ball. In the second place, throwing with a big motion is hard. It's one thing to wind up with a little baseball. But a football is more difficult to grip. If you wave your arm around, it's harder to keep control of the ball.

So I'm going to show you a really simple way to throw. It's a style that takes very little arm action because it uses the natural power you can gain from turning your body. It's easy to learn, and I guarantee it will help you. And I'll tell you a quarterback today who throws the ball this way. Dan Marino.

Every pass you throw is another chance to practice your motion. Even when I was just warming up, I used to carefully cock my shoulder under my chin and throw with the correct motion. I advise you to do that, too. Never be mentally lazy. Use the correct motion on every pass you throw, and then it will come naturally to you under pressure in the big game.

Maybe the best passer playing right now. You ever watch him throw the ball? No wind-up. Just bring it up behind the ear and throw it. It's super quick.

Dan got into it for the same reason I did. When I was a kid, it was my brothers who said, "No wind-up. Throw from the ear." With Marino, it was his dad: "Throw from the ear."

The thing is, to throw like this, you have to use your body correctly. It takes some learning. Sometimes a young passer figures, "I've got my own style. Why should I change?" But even a pro can improve himself. We can grow by learning a more efficient way of doing things. Especially when we are young, we should refine our techniques to a finer level, make ourselves as good as we can be. We'll cover the details in the

You have to
learn *touch*.
You have to
learn to lay the
ball out there
easily. Let your
guy catch the
ball comfortably
in stride.

next few pages. But right now I want to mention some general points about passing the ball well.

Touch: One thing a good passer knows is how to lay the ball out as easily as possible for his receivers. A lot of times a young boy will have a strong arm. His coaches and parents and everybody will be telling him, "Wow, what an arm you've got!" Meanwhile, the kid doesn't know when to back off. Even the short passes he slams out with all his might—and bounces them right off his receivers.

Now don't get me wrong. It's nice to be able to put some heat on the ball when you need it. If you're throwing a hook pass 15 yards downfield, for instance, I don't think there is any way you can throw that pass too hard. You want to get it there in a hurry. But imagine a short slant pass. Or a swing pass to a halfback. If the quarterback guns those balls hard, they're just going to bounce off people. You have to learn *touch*. You have to learn when to lay the ball out there easily. Let your guy catch the ball comfortably in stride.

Timing: Another thing a quarterback has to learn is timing. It's one thing to throw the ball accurately. It's another thing to throw it at the right time. Again, many young passers hold on to the ball too long. Their receiver makes a cut. He's open. The quarterback waits to see *how* open. *Then* he throws. And that's too late. By then the defense has seen the receiver and started to react. The guy was open when you threw the ball. But by the time the ball gets there, he isn't open any more.

So you need to work with your receivers. What you want is to have the ball already in the air by the time your receiver turns around. I'm talking about a downfield pass, like a hook or square-out. The ball should leave your hand just as—or even before—your receiver makes his cut. For sure before his head is around. Give him just enough time to see the ball, to draw a bead on it. But get it there quickly, before the defense can recover. That's what good timing means, and the only way to get it is to practice. Learn how long it takes your receiver to run each pattern. Learn just when to throw so the ball doesn't arrive too soon or too late.

Eyes: Now here's something you should make your mind up about right now. Don't be the kind of quarterback who stares right at his receiver from the start of the play until he throws the ball. Even in the pros, you see guys do this. But it's not smart. The defensive guys are watching your eyes. So if you stare at your receiver the whole play, by the time you throw him the ball, half the defense is going to be over there.

There is no reason for this. You don't *need* to look at your receiver the whole way. Say you're throwing a hook pass to your right. After you've practiced the pass two or three times, you *know* where the guy is going and how long it takes him. You don't have to stare at him. So it's just a matter of practice—of developing a good habit. Whenever you throw that pass in practice, make it your business to look somewhere else the first couple of seconds (sooner or later you'll have to learn to read defenses, anyway). So look up the middle. Or off to your left. Then, just about the time you know he has to make his cut, turn around and look at him. Pick him up with your eyes, and throw him the ball. It's really easy. *Do* it.

Mental Checklist: Like every other player, you should go over a mental checklist as you leave the huddle. You want to have your up-coming actions firmly in mind. A suggested list: First, the snap count. Second, the pass pattern—where are your receivers going? Third, your dropback—are you going straight back, or rolling out? If straight back, is it a quick three-step drop, or five steps, or seven? Finally, think of the count again.

Don't be the kind of quarterback who stares right at his receiver from the start of the play until he throws the ball. It's not smart.

165

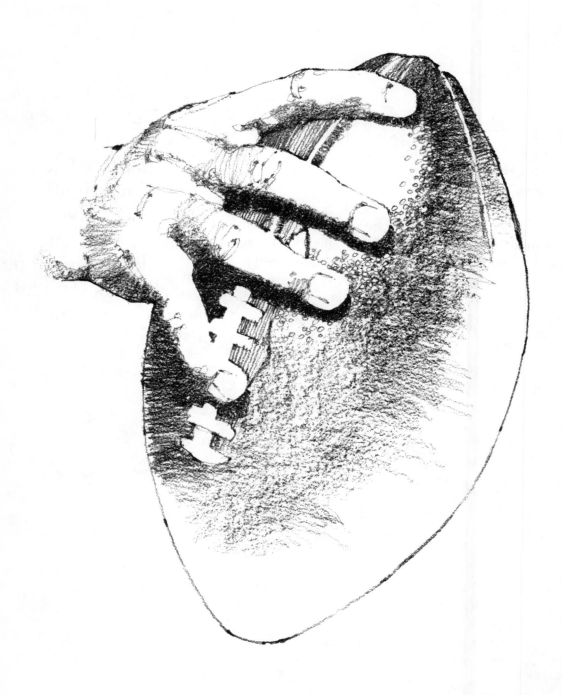

The Grip

To pass the ball accurately, you need a good grip. The picture at the left shows the grip I used. You grab the ball across the laces, and anchor the little finger firmly. Everybody's hand is a different size, of course, and you may still be growing. So you have to make some adjustments. If you're not in high school yet, I think you should use one of the smaller balls. Get a ball small enough so you can grip it roughly like this picture shows. It's better to use a small ball while you are still growing—and develop the right passing motion. If you try to use the big ball before your hand is big enough, you won't be able to grip it right. So get a ball you can grip, and graduate to a bigger ball as *you* get bigger.

Spread Your Fingers: As you grab the ball, spread your fingers as wide as you can—*without* a big strain. The wider your fingers can be, comfortably, the more control you have.

Trigger Finger: Get a relaxed grip across the seam.

Thumb: Reach around the ball opposite the middle finger. The farther toward the middle of the ball you can comfortably reach with your thumb, the more secure your grip will be.

Little Finger: Really hook that little finger hard on the laces. Dig it in there good. Your little finger isn't as strong as the others, and it needs the laces to get a good grip. (Some passers use the ring finger for this; try it both ways.)

Control: The test of your grip is whether you have control of the ball. After you learn the whole throwing motion (in the next pages), then you may have to adjust your grip. You may have to move a bit toward the point of the ball, or a bit toward the middle. What you want is a feeling of solid control as you throw the ball, so the ball goes where you aim it.

It's better to use a small ball while you are still growing—and develop the right throwing motion. Get a ball you can grip, and graduate to a bigger ball as *you* get bigger.

1 Turn your left side to your target, and cock your left shoulder under your chin.

2 Whip your hips and pull your left elbow around. The ball is already behind your ear.

3 As your body turns, your weight shifts from the right side to the left.

4 Weight shifts totally to left side and you reach up high to drive the ball forward with a simple arm motion.

Turning To Throw

Now here is the key to passing. To throw the ball you whip your whole upper body around in a semi-circle. Turning that body gives you power—and keeps the strain off your arm. At first it might feel different from what you are used to. But you'll feel it start to work for you. (In the following, exchange "left" and "right" if you are left-handed.)

Cock Your Shoulder: Start out by facing your left side toward your target. Now cock your left shoulder all the way around under your chin. You have to get your shoulder good and cocked so you can unreel it again. Overemphasize it at first. Your position should be just about like a baseball batter. One thing that helps is to put your left hand on the ball—just pat it gently. That will get your left shoulder cocked under your chin. You wind up looking at your receiver out of the corner of your eye.

Whip Your Hips: As you step to throw, step right at your target—or even step *slightly* to the *left* of your target. Then, as your foot is coming down, start to whip your hips around to the left, like a baseball batter or a golfer. Your body is all coiled up. Now turn your hips and your whole body will start to turn automatically. It's a natural motion.

Pull Your Left Elbow: Your left shoulder is under your chin. Your elbow should be up a bit, pointing out away from you. Now, make your left elbow and your arm and shoulders one solid piece. Whip that elbow around and down. Use it to pull your shoulders around as fast as possible. Whip your elbow—and your shoulders will swing on around, too.

Release The Ball High: You start with the ball about chest high, over on the right side of your numbers (see next pages). As you cock your left shoulder, start the ball straight up, right behind your ear. You don't have to take it backwards, then

Try this motion a little while. You'll feel it start to work for you. It's a completely natural motion. It feels good when you start to get it.

5 Your body keeps right on turning.

1 Left side faces target with left shoulder cocked. Ball is already back.

2 Raise ball straight up behind ear. As left side starts to pull, ball lags behind.

4 Now arm hammers ball forward in simple motion, reaching up for high release.

3 Body is halfway through turn, left elbow is pulling down.

start it forward again. Just raise it straight up—and when the shoulder turn gets far enough along, simply drive your arm up and forward and *release the ball at the highest point.* You want to release the ball nice and high to get it over the defensive guys, so reach way up there as you throw. But don't throw with a true overhand motion, where your arm goes right by your ear—that can strain your shoulder. Instead, as you pull your left elbow and shoulder around, pull them *down* as well. By pulling your left side down, your right shoulder tips upward. You can reach up and release the ball high, even though your arm motion is a comfortable three-quarter style.

The Wrist: The wrist action is something else that comes automatically with this style. Some coaches tell a young passer to turn his wrist in a big counter-clockwise motion and wind up with the fingers pointing out to the right. Maybe that is good for some motions, but not this one. Throwing this way, you want a very simple arm and wrist motion—just as if you were hammering a nail into a wall. There's no need to think much about it. If you use the proper body motion, the wrist will fall into place.

Keep On Turning: After the ball is gone, your body will keep on turning—*if* you have whipped your hips and elbow hard enough, and if you keep your knees flexed. Just let yourself turn out to the left naturally. Sometimes you turn so hard you wind up falling away from the line of scrimmage at an angle. I used to do that. Watch Dan Marino. He does it, too. I don't mean you throw off the back foot—throwing weakly while falling away from the rushers. I mean throwing full-out, with your weight going up to your front leg—then on around. Imagine that straight downfield is 12 o'clock. If you throw a pass out to your left, about 11 o'clock, then a good body turn can turn you away from the line to about eight o'clock.

> You throw by turning your body in a semi-circle, instead of lunging straight ahead.

5 Body keeps turning a full 180°. We see Number 12 on the back now rather than the front.

The Dropback

The way you drop back to pass, and the way you set up, make a big difference in how well you throw the ball.

Before you can pass, of course, you have to drop back into the pocket. The way you drop back to pass—and the way you set up—make a big difference in how well you throw the ball.

When you drop back, I believe you should sprint back as fast as you can go. I know some quarterbacks sort of drift back into the pocket. They run back sideways, with short, choppy, cross-over steps. But I believe you should turn and *run* back there. The faster you can get back, the longer you have to set up and get comfortable. There is less chance of throwing off-balance. Plus, you put distance between you and those big guys chasing you. The main idea is to get away from the rushers, and you want to do it as quickly as you can.

The problem with young quarterbacks is they think they have to keep their head turned downfield so they can watch their receiver. Instead, they keep their whole *body* turned facing the sideline, and now their left leg has to cross over their right in an awkward manner.

The whole thing is a mistake from the beginning. A quarterback doesn't have to keep his head turned to watch his receiver. He *knows* where his receiver is going. It's true that pro quarterbacks (and some in colleges) do have to keep their heads turned—but that's to *read* the *defense*. It's those defensive guys you don't know about. But here's the thing. Young quarterbacks usually don't *have* to read the defense. Their pass plays are simpler than that. So a young passer is free to work on getting the fastest possible dropback. That's what I always stress in our summer camps.

Here's what I tell a young quarterback. I have him face me and take his stance. Then I tell him to turn and run as though there is a $20 bill eight yards straight behind him—and he's in a race for it. What does he do? He turns and *runs*. Darn right he does. So would you. That's the fastest way to get straight back there. You can't win any races by facing sideways and

1 Stance: legs spread, knees bent, weight on balls of feet.

2 "Sit down" as you start. Push off with right foot on quick jab step. Turn left foot toward right sideline.

3 Yank your right elbow and right hip back and around. Drive off hard with left leg. There are three moves here in a split second: Right-Left-Right. Jab-Drive-Stride.

On the dropback a quarterback should turn his back and *run*. That's the fastest way to get back there. You can't win any races by facing sideways and using cross-over steps.

using cross-over steps. I ask all the young quarterbacks to practice the dropback just this way at first. Turn their backs and run. I don't even give them a football. As soon as they get a football in their hands, they try to run back sideways looking downfield. So no ball at first, just turn and run. Once they are comfortable with a full-speed drop, then I give them a ball and have them start to turn their head a bit so they can see downfield. Even to read the defense, usually all you need to see is half the field. That's easy, even when you are turned and running all-out.

Here are some tips for a full-speed dropback:

Stance: Start in a good comfortable stance. Keep your upper body as upright as you easily can. Have your legs spread. Bend your knees and have your weight on the balls of your feet, so you are ready to push off hard (see page 64).

Jab Step: As the center snaps you the ball, first take a small forward step with your right foot—the *jab* step—and push off with it hard. I know some coaches might not like the jab step, but I'm sure it works. It helps you to ride forward with the center to insure getting the snap (see page 84), plus it helps you drop back faster because of the power it gives you. While you push off with the jab step, "sit down" a bit. Let your hips drop a few inches. That gets your weight moving.

Yank Around: As you pull your right foot back, yank your right hip and right elbow back and around, to turn your body.

Drive Off: As you push off with your right foot, your left foot lifts and turns to the right. Then drive off hard with the left leg and the left toes. Really explode with that leg. These first two steps are quick—Right-Left! Jab-Drive! And the first *three* moves are 1-2-3: Jab-Drive-Stride.

First Stride: The first full stride with the right leg is crucial to the dropback. You are pushing with your left leg, and you want your right leg to reach a long way back—and *turn you all the way around*. In your stance, the toes of your right foot are pointed one way; on your first full stride, they are pointed 180° the other way. This opens your hips all the way around, and that's vital. With your hips turned, your left leg can stride through completely on the next step. No cross-over steps.

Second Stride: With your hips turned all the way around and headed straight back, your left leg strides through comfortably. A full running stride. After you have done this many times, and feel comfortable turning all the way around, *then* you can practice turning your head back. Twist back *from the waist up*, and turn your head to look downfield. Your hips are still square to the way you are running, back into the pocket. Only your upper torso turns. If you have trouble with this, do a lot of work with The Twist (see Flexibility, page 48).

THE BACKPEDAL: This is a technique we should mention at least briefly. This is only for older quarterbacks, usually college age and in the pros. Sometimes at these higher levels of the game, you need to see all the way around to your left to read the defense. In that situation, you can't turn your back and run. You have to use the *backpedal*—where you simply *lean back* and scoot your feet backwards while facing straight at the defense. That lets you see the whole field, but it takes more time to get back and it's more difficult to set up. The important tips: (1) Lean back and stand tall while backpedaling. (2) When you want to stop your backpedal, tip your body forward. Stop while leaning forward. (3) At the same time, cock your left side around to face downfield. The hardest part of the backpedal is to get your left shoulder turned all the way around and cocked under your chin before you have to throw.

The first full stride with the right leg is crucial to the dropback. You are pushing with your left leg and you want your right leg to reach a long way back—and turn you all the way around.

175

1On steps three and four, you just coast back easily. Notice that hips are fully turned.

2When it's time to stop, begin to tip forward and start to open the hips.

3Use your left foot as the brake; jam it hard into the ground.

4Stop with weight way forward, and face your left side straight downfield.

The Set Up

After those first two sprinting steps on the dropback, you ease up a bit. Those first two steps are vital for a good dropback. Get your hips turned all the way and drive as hard as you can, and you'll have a fast dropback. But then the next couple of steps you can coast. You can't *keep* accelerating—or how will you stop?

And stopping is a really important part of this whole thing. You have to stop just right, in order to give yourself a good base to throw from quickly.

A lot of quarterbacks stop with their weight on their back leg. In order to throw the ball, they have to redistribute their weight. They have to take two or three steps just to get their themselves moving in the right direction. That's bad for a couple of reasons. First, it takes you a long time to throw the ball if you have to take two or three steps to throw. You always want to throw the ball with just one step. Second, walking forward, you're walking into trouble. The rushers are coming at you. You don't want to move up at them and shorten their trip.

So I believe in stopping your dropback with your *front* leg. I always did the big part of the stopping with my left leg, and I'd end my dropback with my weight way forward. I'd be leaned way out in front of my left leg. My right leg would settle on back behind me to keep good balance—but it didn't take much weight.

After stopping with your weight forward, you just straighten up a bit. Your weight automatically distributes evenly between both legs. You don't have to go digging back and try to pull your weight forward. You already have it where you want it. You're ready to unload.

Naturally, just as you throw the ball you push toward your target with your right leg and follow through onto your left. So only one more thing is needed. How to use your feet when you throw the ball.

After you stop with your weight on your front leg, you just straighten up—and your weight is automatically distributed evenly between both legs. You're ready to throw right now.

Footwork

By bouncing slightly on both feet, you keep your weight moving. You keep your feet lively. Then you can throw faster.

Once you are back where you want to be, you have to get ready to throw—and *stay* ready to throw. You want to be ready to throw in a split instant.

First, straighten up. You have stopped over your front leg. But now you straighten up and distribute your weight evenly between both legs.

Then, start bouncing up and down just a bit—like a baseball infielder taking a little bounce step just as the ball is pitched, or a tennis player skipping his feet as he gets set to receive serve. By bouncing on both feet, you keep your weight moving and your feet lively. Then you can throw faster. You don't usually jump off the ground, but keep yourself loose and moving by bouncing on the balls of your feet.

When you throw, *don't* take a great big step. Your legs are already spread out nicely. All you do is push off with your right foot and take a short step with your left foot directly at your target—or *slightly* to the *left* of your target. Transfer all your weight onto that foot. As your weight moves, pull your left elbow hard and throw the ball. It's all really quick. The pictures below—from bounce to step to release—cover about four-tenths of one second.

Before throwing, keep feet spread, left side to target. Keep your weight bouncing up and down.

To throw, push off with right foot and take a small step with left foot slightly left of target.

Push off with right toe, pull left hip and elbow back, and come through with right arm high.

Throwing On The Run

The main thing is to coil up your upper body before you throw. Even though you're moving right or left, cock that left shoulder under your chin as much as you can.

Many times a quarterback has to throw the ball on the run. Even if you start in the pocket, you may have to scramble and throw while you're moving around. Teams often have their quarterbacks roll out or sprint out to throw the ball, and that means you have to throw on the run most of the time.

Whether throwing while on the run or set in the pocket, the basic mechanics of the upper body are the same. Just practice until you feel comfortable. Here are a few basic tips:

Coil Up: The main thing is to coil up your upper body before you throw. Even though you're moving to the right or left, cock that left shoulder around under your chin as much as you can. Pat the ball with your left hand, to help get you cocked. Otherwise you'll be throwing wide open, with little power from your upper body. Your pass won't have much zip—and you may strain your arm.

Run At Your Target: The best way to throw on the run is to turn upfield before you throw. Even if you are rolling out, first get your depth, then turn upfield. What this does is put pressure on the defense. Now you're running right at them. They have to react to you, come up to tackle you, or you're going to run on them. If they do come up, that should free one of your receivers. I believe the run-pass option is one of the best plays in football, so I advise you to practice it. Be sure to coil that left shoulder before you throw.

Throw Off The Right Foot: If you have a choice, you should throw while stepping off your right foot—and before your left foot has landed. Sometimes you're under pressure and have to get rid of it any way you can, but the best way is to be turned upfield and stepping off your right foot. Try it a few times, and you'll see how it feels.

Throwing on the run, you don't let your left arm wave around loosely. Keep it bent as you see here and use it to pull your upper body around. When you can, you throw as you step off your right foot, but before the left foot hits.

The Receivers

You don't *have* to be big, fast or a tremendous athlete. You can just *make* yourself into a pass receiver.

To play wide receiver, you don't necessarily need great size or speed or athletic ability—though they can all help. The main thing you need is desire—the willingness to work. If you have that, you can *make* yourself into a pass receiver. Look at a guy like Steve Largent of the Seattle Seahawks. Not very big. Not great speed. But an All-Pro. Same with Mike Renfro of the Dallas Cowboys. Or think back to Fred Biletnikoff of the Raiders, who was a Super Bowl MVP. Average size, no blazing speed—but hard workers. Guys who love to practice.

If you want to make it at wide receiver, you have to develop concentration. *Lots* of concentration. It's not really that hard to catch a football. It's only hard when guys are

charging at you from all directions. You hear those footsteps. You know you're going to get hit. But you keep *total concentration* on the football. I like something I first heard from Max McGee, who was a receiver on the great Green Bay Packer teams. "Concentrate," Max said. "They're going to hit you anyway, so you might as well catch the ball."

Concentration means something else, too. It means you concentrate on every part of your job. You keep your mind totally tuned in during practice or during games—and that makes you a dependable target for the quarterback. When he needs to look out there and find you—you are right where you are supposed to be. That's dependability. It makes you very popular with passers, and it comes from concentration.

You should have your mental checklist:
1. Snap count.
2. Pass route.
3. Snap count —or *watch* the snap if it's noisy.

183

The Release

Some guy may line up on your nose and try to keep you from getting downfield. So you need to know how to get a *release*—how to get past that first guy.

To catch a pass, first you have to get off the line of scrimmage. For tight ends, this is usually a problem. Some big guy will line up on your nose—right in front of you—and try to *keep* you from running downfield. In the pros, even a wide receiver will often have a defensive back line up close to play bump-and-run—and this can happen down near the goal line at any level of football. So you need to know how to get a *release*—how to get past that first guy.

The simplest way is shown in the photos below—just stay down low and drive hard past the guy. Dave Casper, long an All-Pro tight end with the Raiders, adds this tip: "Make yourself 'skinny' by dipping your inside shoulder and raising your outside shoulder as you go by the man. This means he doesn't have the whole width of your shoulders to shoot at."

A second way is shown on the opposite page. False-step the guy one way, then come back the other. Usually it's best to stay down low and drive hard after the fake. Drive through the guy's hands. You can also add something else. After false-stepping left, for example, use your right hand to hit him on his shoulder, and "swim" over him with your left arm (see page 216 for the swim technique).

If a defensive player lines up in front of you, you have to release past him. The easiest way is to drive low and hard, go all-out past him.

Stay down low, so you have leverage to drive through the shove he will give you. Explode with your legs and muscle past him.

Another way to get a release is to false-step in one direction, to get your man moving the wrong way.

Then plant your foot and blast back the other way. It's usually good to stay down even lower than you see here.

Driving Them Off

Make him *really* worried. Get him backing up. Get him running back toward the goal line.

O nce you get off the line of scrimmage, you really have to take off. You have to blast downfield as hard and fast as you can. You have to make your defensive man afraid you will blow past him for the long pass.

Remember this: in most defenses, the man covering you has been told, "Don't let that receiver get past you. Never let him get open deep." So that guy is worried about the long pass. What you have to do is—make him *really* worried. Get him backing up. Get him running back toward the goal line.

Sid Gillman has been one of the leading passing coaches in the history of football. This is what he says, "The secret to almost every pass pattern is to sprint hard off the line of scrimmage. Scare that defensive back. Get him turned and running. Then you can make your cut inside or outside. Break it off sharp, and you'll be open."

Of course, if the play tells you to just run right straight past the guy deep, you have to sprint hard off the ball, too. So practice your sprinting start. Practice over and over. Keep your forward lean, with your weight out front. Don't stand right up on your second step. That will slow you down. Keep leaning, and just explode with your legs. Your thigh muscles, your calf muscles, your toes—everything is driving, driving.

As a wide receiver you should probably start in the hunched-over, two-point stance that's popular today. Players have found this gives you the fastest start. To start from this stance, first let your weight suddenly drop down and forward six inches or a foot. The drop of your weight gives you momentum. At the same time, jab back hard into the ground with your rear foot. Really blast with that back foot.

Dropping your weight helps you get a fast start. Then, as you run, stay down low in a combination between a sprinting and hitting position. Staying low, you can run faster and cut sharper. Be sure you don't give away your cuts by suddenly standing up just before you make them. *Stay down low.*

Most wide receivers today use this two-point stance. You can start faster than from a three-point stance.

To get a fast start, first take the stance you see on the page opposite. Then, let your weight drop down and forward while you drive hard off the rear foot. Your arms should pump hard, your leg muscles explode on every stride, and your toes push off full-blast.

Pass Routes

A pass receiver can have a whole bunch of different pass routes that he may run. You want to do different things, keep the defensive back off-balance.

When pass receivers take off down the field, it's not like a street game. The quarterback doesn't say, "OK, everybody go out, and I'll find somebody." Instead, your coach will design *pass patterns*, and every receiver will run a specific *route* within that pattern. The whole pattern should work together, and no two receivers should ever wind up in the same area—unless it's by design.

As a receiver, you should learn all the basic routes that are used to make up pass patterns. It's good to master the ones you see here, plus any others your coach gives you.

To run good routes, you need two things. First, run with a forward lean, almost down in a hitting position, for this reason: standing straight up, your center of gravity is too high. It's hard to make a sharp cut, a high-speed right angle, without rounding it off. If you're up high, you have to almost stop to cut. So stay down low as you run your routes.

Second, master the sharp cut. Practice a million cuts, until you can break one off sharply, like a ball bouncing off a wall. Run up and down the field, cutting hard every third step. *Stay down low* and drive hard *out* of the cut. Coming out of the cut, you want to accelerate and leave your defender behind.

Practice cutting back and forth; right-left-RIGHT (cut), left-right-LEFT, right-left-RIGHT.

Keep cutting back and forth crisply on every third step. Stay down *low* and drive hard on each step.

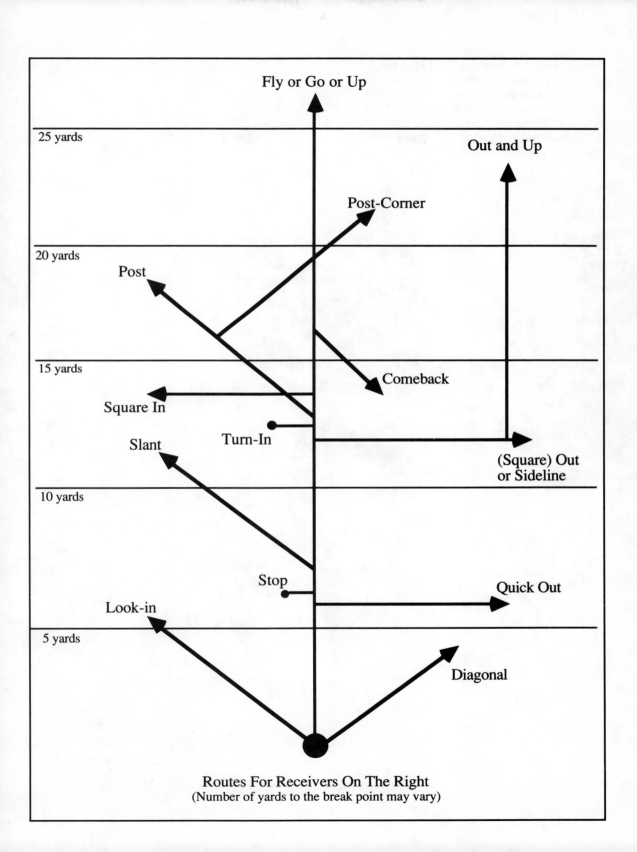

Fly or Go or Up

Out and Up

25 yards

Post-Corner

20 yards

Post

15 yards

Comeback

Square In

Turn-In

(Square) Out
or Sideline

Slant

10 yards

Stop

Quick Out

Look-in

5 yards

Diagonal

Routes For Receivers On The Right
(Number of yards to the break point may vary)

Number 87 has found a dead spot (or seam) in a zone defense, between two linebackers in the short zones and in front of a defensive back in a deep zone. Your coach will help you to recognize the difference between zone and man-to-man, and what patterns to run against each.

Beating The Zone

When you are playing against a man-to-man defense, you need to run your patterns real sharp—and fake out the guy covering you. Running against a zone defense, however, your job is sometimes different. In a zone defense, the defensive guys basically go to the middle of particular areas (or zones) of the field. They are responsible to stay in their zones. They are *not* responsible to stay with any particular receiver—if that receiver leaves their area (deep zones go all the way back to the goal line, however; if you try to go past a guy in a deep zone, he'll turn and run with you).

Against a zone, you can go down the field, run three or four fakes, cut real sharp—and fool nobody. Because nobody is watching you that closely. They're just staying "home" in their zones, waiting until the ball is thrown.

That's why, against a "pure" zone your job changes. You still may run the pattern your play calls for, but instead of running great fakes, what you do is sprint hard off the ball —drive the guys in the deep zones even deeper—then look to find empty spaces in between the defenders. They are staying in their zones, but there are *dead spots* in between the zones. You try to find a dead spot (also called a *seam*).

You can go down the field, run three or four fakes, cut real sharp—and fool nobody. Because nobody is watching you that closely. They're just staying "home" in their zones.

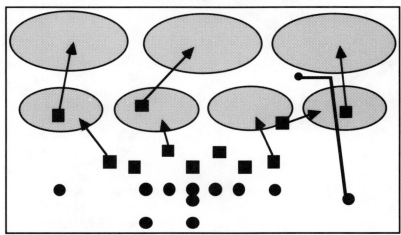

Here is a diagram of the most basic zone defense —the four-short, three-deep zone. You will see this often. One goal of yours will be to find *dead spots* in between zones, where you are a long way from even the closest defender. In this diagram, the wide receiver hooks into a dead spot.

When you're over by the sideline, you really need to concentrate. You have to catch the ball—and (in high school and the pros) you have to keep both feet in bounds. So work on this in practice. Keep your toes in and your eyes locked on the ball.

Concentration

The main thing about catching the ball is: *Concentrate!* Watch the ball. Bore your eyes right into the ball. Pick it up as soon as you can—right from the passer's hand if possible—and watch it all the way into your fingers.

Kids usually think you catch a football with your hands. That's true, in a way. But really you catch a football with your *eyes*. And your *mind*. You watch it so hard, you just concentrate on it so much, that there is no way you can drop it.

Whenever a guy drops a ball, usually there is only one reason. He wasn't really focused on the ball. Either he never really zeroed in on it to begin with—or he took his eyes off it at the last second.

Steve Largent of the Seattle Seahawks is one of the best receivers of our time, and he says, "Sometimes a guy will drop the ball and then he'll tell you, 'Yeah, I saw the ball.' He means he glanced back at some point and saw a brown blur."

That's not good enough. You have to *focus*. You have to lock in on that ball and stare it right down into your hands. "Other techniques don't matter too much," says Largent. "Concentration on the ball is all that really matters. To help my concentration, I don't just look at the *ball*. I focus down until all I see is the *tip* of the ball. That makes me concentrate even more."

Tightening your focus like this can often make you more precise. During warm-ups, for instance, a quarterback can aim his passes at very particular targets on the guy he is throwing to—left shoulder, head, right shoulder, and so on. It helps your accuracy to pick a small target. The same goes for a receiver: the more precisely you focus, the better you'll catch.

Other than that, just practice, practice, practice. Never catch a single ball in a sloppy way—even just tossing it with your friends in the back yard. Watch the ball right into your hands. Stare it in—then tuck it away. If you develop that habit, you'll do it right when you're standing in the end zone.

> Really you catch a football with your *eyes*. And your *mind*. You watch it so hard, you just concentrate on it so much, that there is no way you can drop it.

193

Catching The Ball

A good pass receiver doesn't want to catch *most* passes. He wants to catch *every single pass*. There really isn't any excuse for dropping a pass.

You can catch most of the balls thrown to you without much trouble. But a good pass receiver doesn't want to catch *most* passes. He wants to catch every single pass he can touch.

How many chances does a pass receiver get in a game. Ten? Five? Sometimes *none*. With so few chances, you can't afford to blow one. Plus, there really isn't any excuse for dropping a pass. Catching a football is something you can do *every* time, if you are willing to work at it. And if you can catch every pass, you're going to play a lot.

If you want to be a receiver, work on your speed (see page 54) and practice your patterns. In the passing game, speed and precision really help. If you spend one spring working hard on your sprinting techniques and your pass routes, you'll come back the next fall and dust some defensive backs off. Also, work on catching every single pass—in practice, in games, even just horsing around playing catch.

Catching the football is a skill you can teach yourself. Here are some of the most important tips. If you practice them all the time—if you practice putting your whole mind on the job—then you'll be a good receiver. And here's a plus. If you learn to concentrate fully, it will pay off for you whatever you do. You'll get ahead in class, on the job, everywhere.

CONCENTRATE! Remember, you catch the ball with your eyes, your hands—and your mind. *Concentrate*. Focus on that ball. Watch it *all* the way in—then tuck it away.

Relax Your Hands: The next thing you want is to keep your hands relaxed. A lot of young receivers want to catch the ball so badly, they tense up their hands. Their hands get stiff, and the ball bounces right off. We call it stone hands. So relax your hands. Larry Brown was an All-Pro runner for the Washington Redskins, but he had trouble catching the ball

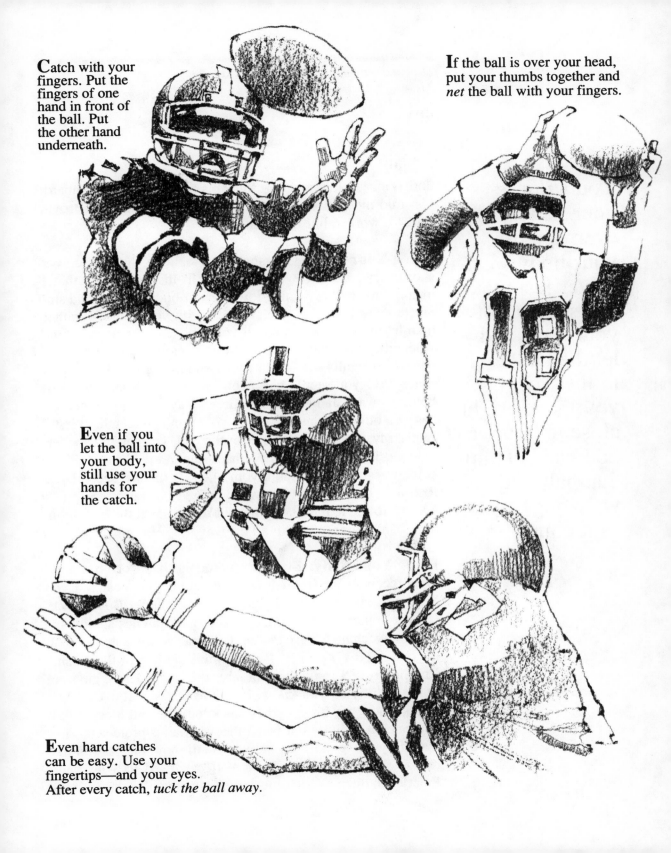

Catch with your fingers. Put the fingers of one hand in front of the ball. Put the other hand underneath.

If the ball is over your head, put your thumbs together and *net* the ball with your fingers.

Even if you let the ball into your body, still use your hands for the catch.

Even hard catches can be easy. Use your fingertips—and your eyes. After every catch, *tuck the ball away*.

You *still* use your hands, even against your body. Never just make a basket out of your arms and let the ball zoom in there. Put your hands right close to your body and clamp that ball with your fingertips as it comes in.

until Vince Lombardi came to be his coach. "Coach Lombardi just told me to watch the ball and relax my hands," Brown said. "It worked like a charm."

Using Your Hands: Personally, I believe that a receiver should try to catch every pass out in his hands. By that I mean, if the ball is coming toward your body, you should still reach out in front and catch the ball with your hands—rather than letting it come in and hit your body. One reason is this: when the ball gets close to you, it can bounce off your pads—especially the front of your shoulder pads. How many times have you seen a ball zoom in to a guy—and then just bounce away? James Lofton, Green Bay's All-Pro receiver, has two other reasons for using your hands to catch. "First," James says, "if you reach out for the ball, you catch it sooner. You get it before a defensive back can get it. Second, if the ball comes all the way into your body, at the last second you lose sight of it. There is no way your eyes can turn down fast enough to see it all the way in. But if you catch the ball out in your hands, you can see it all the way."

Using Your Body: Even if *I* prefer the hand catch, many great receivers do use their body to help with the catch. Lynn Swann used to be that way, and he was a Super Bowl MVP. Charlie Joiner of the San Diego Chargers catches against his body any chance he can—and he has more catches than anyone in NFL history. "I'm not thinking just of the catch," Charlie says. "I'm thinking of *after* the catch. Those guys are going to hit you, you know. If you have the ball out in your hands when they hit you, they can knock the ball loose. But if you catch it against your body, then the ball is protected. They may hit you a good shot, but you'll still hold on." If *you* like to use your body, then be sure to get used to your pads. Practice in them all the time—even when you're out with just

Concentrate totally on every pass you catch, even warming up.

Keep your eyes glued to the ball and catch it with your fingertips.

Then take every single catch and *tuck it in*. Put every pass away.

a couple of friends. Get totally used to them, so the ball won't surprise you when it hits them. Second, even against your body, you *still* use your hands. Never just make a basket out of your arms and let the ball zoom in there. Your arms haven't got any fingers. They can't grab the ball. Put your hands right close to your body and clamp that ball with your fingertips. Use your body only as a backstop.

Reaching Out: If you have to reach out to your left or right, put the fingers of one hand in *front* of the ball. Let the point of the ball hit those fingers, and help out with the other hand underneath (see pictures on page 195). If the ball is over your head, put your thumbs close together and *net* the ball with your fingers. If the ball is low, put your little fingers close together and net the ball with your fingers underneath. Use your fingers. If the ball hits your palms, it might bounce out. Once you have the ball, *tuck it away securely* (see above).

Highest Point: If the ball is high, don't wait for it. Go after it. Jump up and take it at the highest point—just like a basketball rebound. Go up and get it—then tuck it away.

Tight Ends And Backs

A wide receiver has the best chance to go for the long bomb. But there are other guys who may catch the ball even more: tight ends and running backs.

The wide receivers get to make a lot of the flashy catches. A wide receiver has the best chance to go for the long bomb. But there are other guys who may catch the ball even more—guys who get a lot of the shorter passes that make first downs and keep drives going. These guys are the tight ends and the running backs.

The tight end is first of all a blocker. A good tight end is a pretty big guy, and a guy who likes to put his shoulder into people. On many runs, the tight end has the key block.

But the tight end gets to catch his share of the passes, too. Usually he works in the shorter areas—often looking for a dead spot in between zones. He's often working in close quarters, with a lot of traffic all around him. "Those first five yards are a dogfight," says Paul Coffman, the All-Pro tight end for the Green Bay Packers. "There are linebackers all around you, and often the safety is playing up close. You just have to battle your way through."

Your coach may give you specific routes to run. In that case, run them exactly as he tells you. Don't let somebody knock you off your route. If you get bumped, get right back to where you are supposed to be as fast as possible. You have to wind up where your quarterback is expecting you.

If you are playing running back, there is no end to the type of routes you may run. Maybe you just do little flares out of the backfield. But maybe your coach will send you downfield for hooks or sideline patterns. He may even want you to run a fly, to go deep. The main thing is: *learn to catch*. Study the points in this section. Work on it all you can—before and after practice, in the off-season. If you can catch the ball well, you can become a real weapon for your team.

As much as any player on the field, the running back should try to be the *complete football player*. You should be able to run, to block, to receive—and you should work every day on your passing. Do it all. You'll play a lot.

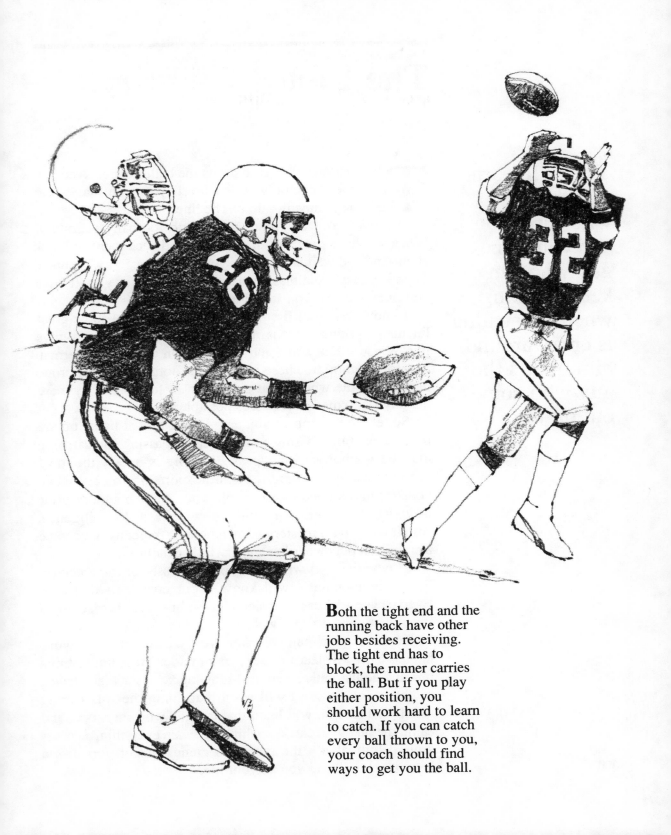

Both the tight end and the running back have other jobs besides receiving. The tight end has to block, the runner carries the ball. But if you play either position, you should work hard to learn to catch. If you can catch every ball thrown to you, your coach should find ways to get you the ball.

The Line

You will learn that the guy who stays cool and calm, the guy who can keep thinking when everything is crazy around him, that's the guy who comes out on top.

The quarterbacks get to throw the ball. The receivers are out there catching. But I'll tell you who makes the passing game possible: The line.

It's really not very hard to throw a football accurately. When you have *time*. When you can stand back there and look all around and wait until one of your receivers gets wide open. Then it's easy. And that's what the line does for you. It buys you time. It keeps you standing up.

I know this from first-hand experience. I had some great linemen working in front of me on the New York Jets—guys like Winston Hill and Randy Rasmussen, and Dave Herman and John Schmidt. These were good football players, proud people, people who would give their all for you. They were the guys who made our passes possible.

So let me tell you: if you are playing in that line, you are the heroes of the passing game. Because passing and catching may be glamorous—but pass *blocking* is one of the most difficult challenges I know about in sports. If you can make yourself into a good pass blocker, you can take a lot of pride in yourself. It takes strength and courage and intelligence. And it takes great mastery of technique. You really have to be a craftsman out there, doing every little detail right.

Maybe the fans will cheer for the passer or the receiver. But your teammates will know. Your coaches will know. Every successful pass is a sign that the line is in there, doing a tough job—and doing it well.

To be a good pass blocker, you will learn good work habits. You will learn to keep calm under pressure, to think fast and adjust, rather than just blowing your stack and trying to batter people. You will learn that doing the smart thing usually wins. You will learn that the guy who stays cool and calm, the guy who can keep thinking when everything is crazy around him, that's the guy who comes out on top. It's a lesson that will help you all your life.

This is perfect form for a pass blocker as he retreats. Stay down low in a good hitting position so you can explode upward and pop your man at just the right instant.

Retreating

The hardest thing about pass blocking is that you have to go backward—and then fire out forward to make your block. First you have to retreat. Then you have to explode on your man. There is only one way to get it down. Learn the right techniques, and then practice long and hard.

To do this right, first you have to learn where your quarterback is going to be. And I mean, *exactly*. Because you have to stay right between your man and the quarterback. You can't get a little to one side and give that rusher a straight line to the passer. Jim Hanifan has been a head coach with the St. Louis Cardinals, and he is one of the most respected line coaches in the NFL. Hanifan says, "The hardest thing I have to teach pass blockers is to stay right between their man and the passer. They just don't believe that being an inch or two off will give their man too much of an advantage. But it will."

Even an inch or two can let the rusher get some leverage on you, and shorten his route to the passer.

So be in the right place, and as you back up, always stay down in a good hitting position. Keep your legs in a power squat, your back straight and your head up. You need to keep that explosive position so you can strike at any moment.

> Stay down in a good hitting position. Keep your legs in a power squat, your back straight and your head up. You need to keep that explosive position so you can strike at any moment.

As you retreat, keep your legs spread to give you balance. Also, keep your feet chopping up and down rapidly—for the same reason that the quarterback bounces up and down while waiting to throw. It keeps your weight moving and your feet lively so you can strike out at any instant.

203

Keep those legs really spread out. Then he can't knock you sideways. And when you pop up into his chest, as this blocker is doing, drive both those forearms up to knock him up and back. Remember, up through high school you can't use your hands to push like they do in college and the pros. So keep your hands in and hit with your shoulders and forearms.

The Hit

After the pass blocker has backed up a couple of yards, he has to stop and make a stand. You can't just keep backing up until you're in the quarterback's lap. So after two or three steps back, you have to stop and pop the man coming at you. You have to bring him to a halt, or he'll roll right over you to the quarterback.

"Be sure you're down good and low," says Dan Dierdorf, the Cardinal All-Pro who is now a television commentator. "You have to have your legs bent, your back straight and your head up. Then wait until the guy gets good and close to you—and unload on him."

Wait until the last second to give your hit. Don't fire out too early, when you're too far away, and *miss* the guy. You have to wait until he's so close you know you can't miss. Then explode your legs and hit him a shot upward into his chest. Drive both forearms up as you hit. Wham! You hit him your very best shot. Up until now you've been retreating, giving ground. But at the instant you meet, you want to be exploding forward. If you aren't, he's got a head start, and he's just going to drive right over the top of you.

As hard as you hit the guy, however, you still have to be under control. You can't hit the guy a big shot and then fall down. He'll just waltz in. So you wait until he's really close to you, and then you hit him a short, hard one. Pow! Like a short inside punch in boxing. Or a karate jab. You're under control. You stay within yourself. You don't overextend.

One thing that will help you a lot is this: remember to keep your feet spread out wide. Keep a good wide base underneath you. If you're thinking about keeping those feet spread, and you're thinking about staying crouched way down low, you'll see you can pop upwards with a lot of power and still keep yourself under control. The only thing is, to do this right, you need great leg strength. Work hard on those legs so you have the strength to explode at your man.

Wham! You hit him, and then you pull right back down into your hitting position. Hit and recoil. Hit and drop back ready to hit again.

Here the blocker is in perfect position just after hitting his man. He has hit with his forearms and shoved back again. As you push back, you can get your arms out this far, but only briefly, and not much farther, by current high school rules. In high school, as we've said, you can't hit or push with your hands.

The Recoil

On a quicker pass, your coach will ask you to block differently. He might want you to fire out straight into your man—which is called *aggressive pass blocking*. Boom! one shot and the ball is gone. Or he might want you to duck down and cut the guy's legs out with a chop block so the quarterback has a clear passing lane for a second.

On a regular pass, however, you need to give the quarterback time. That's why, once you've hit your man on regular pass blocking, you have to get off him and get ready to hit again. You don't want him to grab you. "You have to stay away from that rusher," says Jon Kolb, a tackle on the great Pittsburgh Steeler teams of the 1970s. "You have to hit him and get away again. If he grabs you, he can throw you."

So you hit—and *recoil*. You hit the guy a hard shot in the chest. You bang those forearms up there hard—and you shove off with your forearms and fists. Bounce back and settle down into a good hitting position right away. This takes practice, but when you do it, you've got him. Now you can hit him again. Or you can go low and chop his legs out. Or you can just move with him and screen him off if he tries to run around you. The key is to hit and recoil.

> You bang those forearms up there hard—and you use that power to bounce back off him. Bounce back and settle down into a good hitting position right away.

Wait till the guy is right on top of you, then explode your legs and hit him a shot in the chest.

Hit both forearms hard up into his chest and use that power to drive yourself backward again.

Get back and set up to hit him again. Stay down even lower than this, in the hitting position.

PART FIVE

Stopping The Pass

The quarterback looks out at a linebacker and a defensive back—key parts of any pass defense. But the best pass defense is a big rush by the defensive line. That makes life easy for the linebackers and backs.

Stopping The Pass

I'll tell you the best pass defense I ever played against. Mother Nature. That's right. She put up the best defense I ever had to deal with.

This was in Buffalo. Nice open air stadium. It was raining like a waterfall and the wind was blowing like you wouldn't believe. A 30- or 40-mile-an-hour cross-wind. I'd throw the ball out there, and the wind and rain would just knock the pass straight to the ground. The first ten passes I threw, I had the guy open, and I just couldn't get the ball to him. It was like throwing into a wall. Neither team completed a pass in that game until late in the fourth quarter.

I'll tell you how bad it was. My father and my brother Frank had driven up from Pennsylvania to see the game. A few minutes into the first quarter they just got up and left. People called out to them, "How can you leave? That's Joe out there." Frank said, "Hey, he's working. If he wasn't working, he wouldn't stay here either." He was right, too.

Talking ordinary pass defense—pass defense run by people instead of by nature—that's something else. The key to a good pass defense is to put pressure on the passer. If you let the quarterback just stand back there and find somebody, he's going to eat you up.

Just imagine that you're out on the field, you and your buddy. I tell your buddy to run all over the field, anywhere he wants, as long as he wants. Do you think you can cover him forever? No way. It doesn't matter how good you are. If the quarterback can just wait until the guy gets open, he's going to complete the pass.

That's why the Chicago Bears blitz all the time. You want to pressure the quarterback. And that's why the old Pittsburgh Steeler defense and the great Dallas Doomsday defense were so tough. They didn't even have to blitz. Their four front guys could get to you by themselves. That left seven men back to cover the receivers—which is very tough pass defense.

211

This is good pass rush technique. The rusher's head is up and he is going to wrap his arms around the quarterback up high—where he might knock the ball loose.

The Rush Line

If you're up front in the rush line, you are the guy who can hurt a passing game. You and the linemen next to you. If you can get a good pass rush by yourselves, all the linebackers and defensive backs can stay back and cover the receivers. It's going to be a long day for the other team's passer.

When I think about pass rushers, I remember Mr. Ernie Ladd, who played for the Chargers and the Chiefs. Ernie was six feet ten inches and 300-plus pounds. The first time I played against him, he hit me a heck of a lick—just pounded me. He's on top of me, I'm looking out the earhole on the side of my helmet, seeing stars, mostly, and Ernie says, "Don't worry, Broadway. I'm not going to hurt your knees. I'm going to hit you high." I thank you for that, Ernie.

Now, even if you're not 6-10, you can still get a good pass rush, still upset the quarterback. Here's what you do. First, key on that blocker right in front of you (see page 130). If he backs up—if he sets back to block for a pass—you charge like mad. You were charging anyway, to penetrate and stop a run. Now you just keep coming as hard as you can— and try to hit him before he can set up.

For many good pass rushers, that's all it takes. Joe Klecko is an All-Pro nose tackle for the New York Jets, and this is his style. "I'm a big power rusher," Joe says. "There's not a lot to it. I'm going to run you over my best way."

This is OK if you are bigger or stronger than your opponent. But if you aren't, then you need some technique. You've got to use your head. If you just charge blindly into your blocker, and churn away getting nowhere, that's just what the blocker wants. You and he are dancing, and meanwhile the quarterback has all the time in the world.

You have to remember that pass rushing is not just a personal contest between you and your blocker. This isn't glorified arm wrestling. The idea is to get the quarterback. The idea

Pass rushing is not just a contest between you and your blocker. The idea is not just to see which of you is stronger or which of you is tougher. The idea is to get the quarterback.

213

The Rip Move

You've got to be strong for this, but you see a lot of players use it these days. It gets you good leverage on the blocker.

Here's one move you can work on. You've got to be strong for this, but you see a lot of players use it these days. It gets you good leverage on the blocker, and it's easier than trying to run right over him.

This is called the *rip* move. What you do is charge at your man, give him a little juke one way and then drive under him the other way. Jack Youngblood, the all-time defensive end who has just retired from the Los Angeles Rams, was great at this move. "Say you want to drive past his right side," Youngblood says. "You drive your *right* arm across in front of him—and up under his right side. Then you rip your right arm up under his armpit. You lever him up in the air."

The rip gives you two chances. First, you may knock the guy off-balance. Then you can just shove him off—shed him and charge the quarterback. But at the very least, you have gotten out to the side of the blocker—he's no longer right in front of you like a big roadblock—and you have him levered up where he can't drive you. Now just dig in and drive through him. Blast him hard as you rip under him, then just keep on going. Even a few steps puts you in position to give the quarterback trouble.

To do the rip correctly, first you have to get the guy off-balance. Fake one way, then come across and drive your arm up under his other arm.

Don't just stick your arm out. Drive your shoulder hard up under his shoulder and rip your arm upwards. Try to knock him off-balance and bull past him.

When you go for the rip, you have to go all-out.
Slam your shoulder up under him, rip that arm up hard,
and drive past him. Don't do the move in one spot. Rip
under him while you *blast past* him. Drive *through* him. You
have to get to the quarterback, and you can't slow down to
wrestle with the man in front of you.

The Swim Technique

> You wheel your arm over the guy. You "swim" right by him. It's great when it works, but if you don't get past him clean, you're way up high and he's down in a good position under you.

Here's another move you see a lot. It's called the swim technique. Defensive linemen use this move. So do pass receivers when they are trying to get a release past a guy right in front of them. If you do it right, you can get by your man quick and clean.

To do the swim, you start off with a quick fake to the right, let's say, just a head fake and a quick juke step. Now reach out with your left arm. Swing it hard and hit the guy on his right shoulder. Since you faked the other way, he'll be starting that way. Now you bang him on the shoulder and knock him even farther in the same direction. Plus you grab on. Grab his shoulder pad or jersey.

Merlin Olsen made the Hall of Fame as a defensive tackle. "Once you can grab that shoulder," Olsen says, "you're in good shape. You pull the shoulder toward you and down. That pulls you past the man. And you pinwheel your right arm up and over so the blocker can't hit you on that side. If you do it right, you're past him."

You wheel your arm over the guy. You "swim" right by him. It's great when it works, but if you don't get past him clean, you're way up high and he's down there in a good position under you. Says Jack Youngblood, "They can really put it on you. Your whole side is exposed, and they can really put you on your ear."

(When an offensive pass receiver uses the swim, he has to forego the grab. If you are a tight end, say, you can usually get away with banging the guy's shoulder, but if you grab him, the man in the zebra suit will probably call it.)

To do the swim right, some coaches think you need to be taller than your blocker, and that may be right. If you're having trouble with the swim, here's another technique. Reach across in front of him, say with your right arm, and grab *his* right arm—the back of his upper arm. If you can get that grip, you can pull yourself right past the guy.

First you fake one way. Say you fake right. Then reach out with your left arm and get a good grab (top picture). Pull his shoulder down and toward you—and swim over him with your right arm (bottom). Do the whole move while charging ahead. Don't just stand in one spot and dance with the guy.

Hands High

Get those hands up. When all the rushers have their hands in the air, it's mighty tough on the passer.

A lot of times you'll see young players trying to do a swim. First they'll be faking back and forth for a while, then they'll be pulling and tugging and hauling on their blocker. While all this is going on, the passer is picking out a receiver and throwing the ball.

You can't get so wrapped up in battling your blocker that you forget what you're trying to do. Maybe he's blocked you once or twice. Don't get frustrated. Don't get so mad at your blocker that all you want to do is stand there and beat on him. Remember your target is the quarterback. Keep cutting your eyes to the quarterback. As for the blocker, get *rid* of him and go do your job.

One final word on pass rushing. When that quarterback gets ready to throw the ball—*get your hands up in the air*. Maybe you were totally blocked and never got off the line of scrimmage. Still get those hands up. When all the rushers have their hands in the air, it's mighty tough on the passer. The Dallas Cowboys are an excellent team at this. They usually get a lot of hands up there when the quarterback winds up. You get yours up, too, and you'll bat some important passes down.

Even if all the rush men are blocked, they can still make it hard to pass. All they have to do is get their hands up in the air when the quarterback tries to pass. If they raise their hands and jump, they clog up the passing lanes. Concentrate on this and do it on every pass play.

If you get your hands up, you may block the pass.
Just as important, you may make the quarterback
recock or throw the ball off-target.

The Linebackers

You start by reading your keys. You have to tell if it's a pass play right away. If you're slow getting your read, then you'll be slow getting back on your coverage.

The linebackers are crucial to a good pass defense. They have to play it smart. One of the smartest I played against was Bobby Bell of the Kansas City Chiefs. He's in the Hall of Fame now, and I can see why. He was always tough for us, especially when we played them in the AFC Championship in 1970.

We got down right on their goal line one time, and we had a play put in just for Bell. He was so smart that we tried a double whammy on him. Usually, if you faked a pitchout and then handed off on a quick trap up the center, Bell would ignore the outside fake and close right down to the inside and eat up the trap. So our play was to fake the pitch, then *fake* the trap, then throw out in the flat on Bell's side. He was supposed to bite on the second fake. But did he? Nope. Too smart. He was still out there. I had nothing to do with the ball and wound up under an avalanche of tacklers. On a frozen field. And I was the one who had thought up the play.

You've got to be smart to play linebacker. You start by reading your keys. You have to tell if it's a pass play right away. If you're slow getting your read, then you'll be slow getting back on your coverage. They'll beat you.

You read the same way we've already said. Watch through the linemen into the backfield. If the linemen back up—Pass! Get to your assignment, and watch for a draw play or screen pass as you back up. "Your first three steps," says Denver's Pro Bowler Karl Mecklenburg, "you keep your eyes on that backfield. You're running back to your spot, but you watch the ball."

There is only one way to learn to read the offense. Practice. You have to practice so much, and be so alert, that the first moves by the offense trigger your first moves almost automatically. Maybe you'll hear some kid say, "I don't like to practice. I'm a game day player." I'll tell you what. You need to practice to play on game day.

PHOTO: HERB WEITMAN

The Drop

A linebacker can't afford to have tunnel vision. You have to see many things at the same time.

Most of the time up through high school, you'll be playing zone defenses. In a man-to-man defense, you get one receiver to cover and you run with him everywhere. But in a zone, you get one specific area of the field to cover. As soon as you read pass, your first assignment is to run back to the middle of your zone.

For a linebacker, dropping back to your zone takes some work. First of all, you have to run backwards while looking forwards. Tom Cousineau of the Cleveland Browns, one of the NFL's best linebackers, says, "As you drop back, first you check for a draw or screen. Then you watch the quarterback. Read his eyes. See where he wants to throw. Finally, look around and see the receivers. Watch for the receivers who can get into your zone and hurt you."

Playing linebacker, you can't afford to have tunnel vision. You have to see many things at once. You also have to hurry. Says Jack Ham, the Steeler all-timer, "You have to get back to your zone right away. Get back and turn and get set up in a good position. The worst thing is to still be drifting back when the quarterback throws. You're drifting back off-balance and you can't react. So get back quickly and get set."

To get a good drop, you have to read your keys right away, then turn and sprint to your zone.

Keep your head turned back to watch the quarterback. When you get to your zone, slow up.

Hurry hard so you have time to get to your zone, then turn and get in a good football position.

Taking your drop, you have to keep your head on a swivel. Watch the quarterback but keep track of the nearby receivers, too. You have to know which receivers can get into your zone and give you trouble.

Playing Man-to-Man

The key to this—for a linebacker—is to get a good jam on your man. Maybe you'll be covering a tight end, maybe a back. But the first thing you do is: *jam* the guy.

Some guys get the wrong idea about a zone defense. Since it's not a man-to-man, they just ignore everybody and stand in the middle of their zones. But that's not good enough.

As a linebacker, you play in a short zone. Now it's true that you don't chase some guy if he runs *through* your zone. You shouldn't run all the way across the field with him. Don't *leave* your zone to chase a man—unless the quarterback throws him the ball.

On the other hand, if somebody comes into your zone, you *do* cover him. Don't just be a spectator while he catches the ball. He's in your area, so get up on him. After a while, you'll begin to play the zone even smarter. Maybe you'll look around and see, "Nobody is threatening my zone." Maybe the wide receiver went deep, the tight end is on the other side of the field, and no back came out. So nobody is threatening your zone. That means you can look around and start to edge over toward your buddies. Try to see who needs help.

You may also have to play man-to-man sometimes. Maybe several guys are blitzing. Maybe the offense is down near your goal. Whatever, your coach may ask you to play man-to-man. They key to this—for a linebacker—is to get a good jam on your man. Maybe you'll be covering a tight end, maybe a back. But the first thing you do is: *jam* the guy. Give him a good shot with your hands in the chest and knock him off-stride. He may be faster than you, so you have to slow him down right away. And you usually try to bump him to the outside and force him to *stay* outside.

Says Jack Ham, "The easiest throw for the quarterback is a quick shot right over the middle to the tight end or a back. It's like throwing darts. So don't give him a chance to cut inside you. Step right up and jam him. With a back, go meet him in the backfield. Slow him down and force him outside."

Number 50 is playing to the inside. A good linebacker like Jack Ham says, "Never drift back and let the receiver run right at you. Then he has a two-way go. He can break right or left, and you're in trouble. Always step up and jam him, then take away one side, usually his inside." Force him toward the sideline (see page 233).

The Blitz

Then there's the fun way to play pass defense. Blitz. Go get the quarterback. On a blitz a linebacker or defensive back rushes in to help pressure the quarterback. There are really only two things you need to know about the blitz.

First, don't just shoot in helter-skelter. Your coach will design your blitz and you will have a specific *lane* to fill. Blitz through that lane. If you all rush to the right, who's going to mind the store over on the left? You want to stay coordinated with your buddies and keep a fence around the quarterback. You want to block his vision, have somebody plugging up each passing lane, and close off any escape routes. Plus, if it's a run, you will have somebody covering each gap. You won't bunch up all together and leave empty lanes for the runner to waltz through untouched.

Second, once you start to blitz, *go like mad*. Get it in your mind that nobody is going to stop you. Throw guys, run over guys, *jump* over guys. Whatever you have to do. Get in there. Your defensive backs are back there without any help, and the offense may burn you for a big gain or TD.

Get it in your mind that nobody is going to stop you. Throw guys, run over guys, *jump* over guys. Whatever you have to do to get the quarterback.

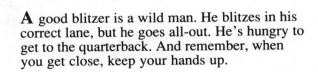

A good blitzer is a wild man. He blitzes in his correct lane, but he goes all-out. He's hungry to get to the quarterback. And remember, when you get close, keep your hands up.

227

The Secondary

Eric Wright says, "If they catch it short on you, you can come up and make the tackle. Then you get to line up again. But if they catch it behind you, you just go sit on the bench."

The best pass defense may be a big rush on the quarterback. But you need good defensive backs to shadow those pass receivers. A really good defensive back can drive passers and receivers crazy.

One of the best I ever played against was Pat Fischer, a cornerback for the Cardinals and Redskins. He was just a little guy, 5-9 and 170, but he proved you can play with brains and desire. I remember one time when Fischer came right up to play bump-and-run with Richard Caster. Now Caster was 6-5 and 230, and I loved that. Right away I called an audible to throw to Caster. I figured he's got to out-muscle and out-jump that little Fischer. But Fischer was a tough little guy. He got a good jam on Caster and never let him off the line. I had to eat the ball. Next play: same situation. I still liked it. I called the same audible again. And danged if Fischer didn't jam Caster up again. He was tough and he was smart. Maybe he was little, but he played big.

When *you* start thinking about pass defense, here is the most important thing to remember: stop the deep pass. Eric Wright, Pro Bowl cornerback for the San Francisco 49ers, says, "Don't ever give them the long bomb. It could mean six points right now. If they catch it short on you, you can come up and make the tackle. Then you get to line up again. But if they catch it behind you, you just go sit on the bench."

A lot of young players feel bad if their receiver catches even a short hook pass. So they get overaggressive, come up too fast—and get burned deep. So learn patience. Play it smart. Force the offense to march down the field on a series of short plays. That's very tough for them to do. If they have to run 11 or 12 plays before they can score, usually they will foul up. Some offensive guy will jump offside, or hold, or fumble. If you make them run a bunch of plays, usually they will make a mistake and stop themselves.

If you are close enough, go for the ball. Once the ball is in the air, the defensive back has an equal right to it. If you are going for the ball, you can hit the receiver accidentally, but you can't shove or grab him on purpose.

You have to practice a lot
to get a good backpedal.
Work hard to make your
legs strong. Sit back into it,
shove back with your legs,
and stay low. Build up
speed with practice. Also
practice backpedaling—
and then turn and run full
speed in the same direc-
tion. Or break off to the
left or right. Or charge
straight back toward
the line again.

The Backpedal

If you want to play defensive back, you have to learn to do something that's not really natural. You have to learn how to run backwards. As a defensive back, you spend a lot of your time doing your *backpedal*, for two reasons. First, you want to see as much of the play as you can, and you want to be ready to react to things that happen in front of you. Second, on a pass play, you want to be moving back toward your own goal line. You want to keep the receivers in front of you so they can't catch the long one.

Of course, on some plays you eventually have to turn and run full-out. If your receiver is trying to get past you, you can't let him catch up to you while you are still in your backpedal. He'll blow right by you. So before he gets to you, you have to turn and go.

But the longer you can backpedal, the better. In the backpedal you can see and react. Once you turn your back and run, it's hard to stop and come back up for a short pass, or for a draw play or scramble by the quarterback. So you should work on your backpedal a lot. The main thing is to stay down low, down in a good hitting position. This keeps your balance and lets you react quickly.

Try to stay in the backpedal as long as you can. In the backpedal you can see and react. Once you turn your back and run, it's hard to stop and come back up.

As you backpedal, stay down low in a good hitting position—and be sure to keep your head up.

Your feet should skim as close to the ground as possible—without catching in the grass.

When it's time to charge forward again, *lean* way forward, plant that back foot—and drive *hard!*

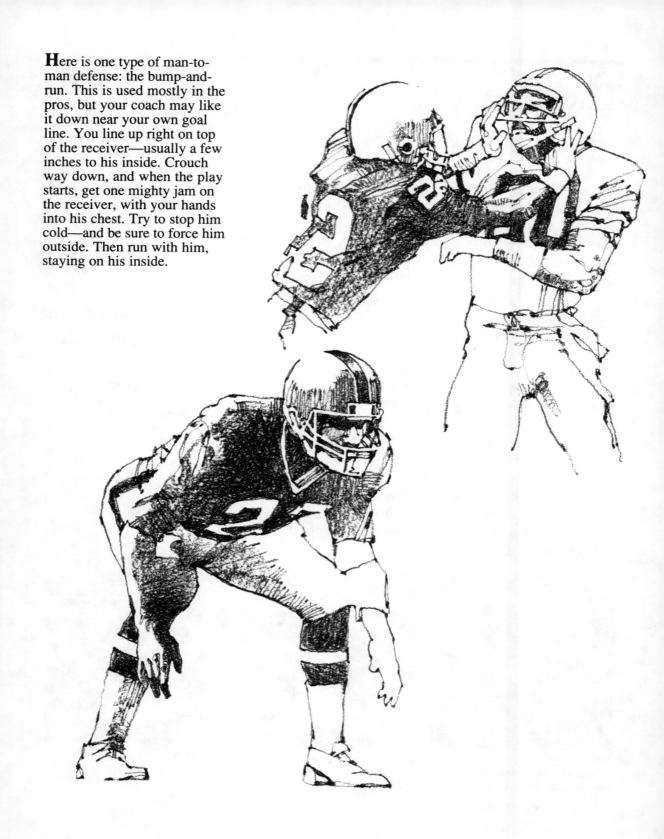

Here is one type of man-to-man defense: the bump-and-run. This is used mostly in the pros, but your coach may like it down near your own goal line. You line up right on top of the receiver—usually a few inches to his inside. Crouch way down, and when the play starts, get one mighty jam on the receiver, with your hands into his chest. Try to stop him cold—and be sure to force him outside. Then run with him, staying on his inside.

Man-To-Man

During your early years in football, your coach may not ask you to play much man-to-man. It's usually safer for a team to play zone, with three guys in deep zones to stop the long passes. But still it's a good idea to practice man-to-man coverage. It makes you quick and alert. And sometimes you'll have to play it—maybe when your linebackers all blitz, or sometimes down near the goal line.

Playing man-to-man, your first thought is the same as for all pass defense. Don't let the guy deep. Don't give up the bomb. The next thing is: overplay the guy to one side, usually the inside. Says San Francisco's Eric Wright, "In a true man-to-man, you have no help inside. If the guy gets inside you, he can run all the way across the field. So what you want to do is keep the guy on the outer edge of the field, between you and the sideline. That sideline is all the help you've got."

You usually line up seven or eight yards downfield—and one yard *inside* your man. As he runs downfield, you backpedal. If he veers toward you, keep sliding over so you are still inside him. Don't let him get right in front of you. If you stay on his inside, and he tries to *break* inside, you already have a head start on him. As Wright says, "Hold onto your inside technique. If you're already inside and he cuts in there, you should be able to drive on him and at least tackle him after the catch. He won't get away from you cross field."

With you inside, of course, he can break *outside*, toward the sideline. But that's what you want. First, the sideline helps you. The receiver has to stay on the field to play the game. Second, throwing the ball out wide is harder on the quarterback. He has to throw a long way—and if the ball is a little late or a little soft, you may drive up and get it. Even if the pass is complete, you and the sideline should be able to stop the receiver. That's why defensive backs (and linebackers, too) usually play their men from the inside—and try to force them out toward the "twelfth defender," the sideline.

Defensive backs (and linebackers, too) usually play their men from the inside—and try to force them out toward the "twelfth defender"—the sideline.

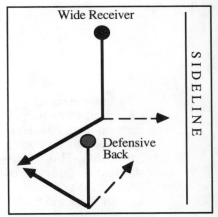

On normal man-to-man, play a little inside of the receiver. Then if he breaks inside, you have a head start to cut him off. If he breaks outside, you have farther to go, but the sideline helps you contain him.

Playing Zone

You have to be careful if a receiver comes across into your area in front of you. If you run up to cover him, another receiver may cross behind you deep.

We've already talked about playing a zone—from the standpoint of a linebacker (see page 22). Many of the same points apply for defensive backs. You cover an area, not any particular man. You move to cover closely any man who comes into your area. If no one is threatening your area, you look to help out your buddies.

But a couple of more points need to be made. First of all, defensive backs often have deep zones to cover, rather than short ones. When they do have the deep zone, their primary responsibility is to prevent the long pass. Especially playing zone, we should *never* let them have the big play. This means you have to be careful if a receiver comes across into your area in front of you. If you run up to cover him, another receiver may cross behind you deep. Don't come up unless you *know* that no one else can hurt you long.

Another thing: you play zone defense—and really all pass defense—based on *down* and *distance* and *score*. If it's third and 20, you can let them have a ten-yard hook. Don't jump on that too quickly. But if it's third and ten, and they are driving down close for the winning score, play it tougher. Don't just *give* them the short one then. Fight them for every yard.

We saw the basic four-short-three-deep zone on page 191. Here is another zone you see sometimes. This has five short zones and only two deep. It is very good against short and middle-range passes. But with only two guys deep, it can be dangerous on long passes—especially if the offense has more than one fast receiver.

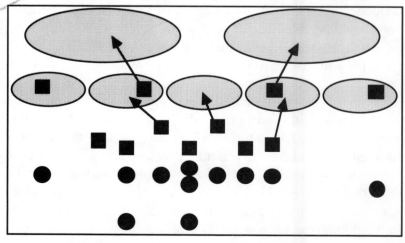

Playing a zone defense, you really have to hurry back to your zone. At the snap of the ball, your first step is back. Then if you read pass (if the offensive line backs up to pass block), just keep running to your zone. As you run, keep your head turned to watch the receivers—and especially the quarterback's eyes.

You have to drive on the ball with everything you have. Once the ball is in the air, come as hard as you can. Even if you can't get the pass, you can knock the ball loose from the receiver, or hit him short of a first down.

Driving On The Ball

There's one thing a defensive back really has to be geared up for. Maybe you're backpedaling while playing man-to-man. Maybe you're back in a deep zone. But when that quarterback puts the ball in the air, boy, you have to go *get* it—full speed.

It doesn't matter what your responsibility used to be. Once that ball is in the air, your responsibility is to go after it as fast as you can. So whatever else you're doing, you have to be all charged up for an explosive change of direction at any instant. It's like you're running one way—covering some guy, or heading back to your zone—but in your mind you are down in a sprinter's stance. You're ready to just charge off after the ball, wherever it goes.

Sometimes it's hard for young players to understand this at first. They're covering a guy, the ball is thrown, they come up all right—but they don't *explode* up. They don't plant a foot and *drive* toward the ball like their life depended on it. That's what you have to do. You have to *drive on the ball*, charge toward it with all you've got. If you go at it all-out, maybe you'll get a hand on it. Or maybe you'll arrive just after the ball—but hit the receiver so hard, he'll drop it.

I remember Al Atkinson, our middle linebacker. In Super Bowl III, the Colts were moving in the first quarter. They were down close to a score that would have put them 7-0 ahead. They tried a hook pass—and Atkinson drove toward that ball with all his might. He leaned way out and just did barely tip the ball. Maybe that doesn't sound like much. But the ball bounced off the receiver's pads and way up in the air. Our cornerback, Randy Beverly, intercepted. Even a tiny fraction of an inch can change a game. So drive on the ball with all your might.

Even if the pass is to the other side of the field, take off full-speed. You've got to get over there and help out. Clean up on a tackle or pick up a fumble. Go get the *ball*.

> You have to *drive on the ball*, charge toward it with all you've got. If you go at it all out, maybe you'll get a hand on it. Or maybe you'll hit the receiver so hard, he'll drop it.

237

PART SIX

The
Kicking
Game

PART SIX
The Kicking Game

Sometimes, when we think about playing football, all we think about is offense and defense. We think, "Do I want to play fullback or linebacker?" But here is something to remember: somewhere between 20% and 25% of the time during an average football game is devoted to something *besides* regular offense and defense. That's right. Between 20% and 25% of the time is devoted to the *kicking game*.

That's how important the kicking game is. In a typical pro game, there are 25 or 30 kicking plays. And kicking plays are usually very important. Every place kick can mean points—one point for the extra point and three for the field goal. And most punts move the ball 30 or 40 yards downfield. That's a big switch in field position. And think about a long kick runback, or a punt block, or when a return man fumbles the ball away. All these are plays that can turn a game around.

That's why the kicking game is so important. In our Super Bowl season, for instance, the kicking game was a big factor. First, we had the best defense in the league. Second, we had a great field goal kicker—Jim Turner. That meant we could play a little conservatively on offense. When we got down close, we didn't have to get too hungry and make mistakes. We could count on Turner to get us field goals—and our defense to make them stand up. I remember there was one stretch of about five games in there where I didn't throw a single touchdown pass. In the dressing rooms after the game, I'm having to defend myself against reporters who wonder why I'm not throwing any touchdowns. "Hey," I told them, "we just won five in a row. Who cares how we win?"

See, they didn't understand the importance of the kicking game. But you should. And you should try some kicking, punts and place kicks both. There's no reason you can't be a good kicker. Plus, when you play on kicking teams, hustle hard and take pride in being a good blocker and tackler. Every kicking down is a chance for you to make a big play.

240

PHOTO: VERNON BIE

The Punt

> The punt buys you field position. If your punter is backed up in his own end zone—and then just boots it out of there past the fifty—it feels great.

The punt buys you field position. It's a lousy feeling if your punt return guy fouls up—maybe bobbles the ball and stumbles around and gets caught back inside his ten. But if your punter is backed up in his own end zone—and then boots it out of there past the fifty—it feels great.

In fact, I'll tell you one of the most amazing feelings I ever had in a football game. I'm standing on the sideline on fourth down. We've got the ball on our own one-yard line and our punter, Steve O'Neal, is way back in the end zone. The next thing I know here comes this ball soaring through the sky. I couldn't believe it. It was up in the air so *long*. Denver's return man just turned and started running, but it went way over his head. By the time it stopped rolling, you know where it was? On their *one-yard* line. Unbelievable. A 98-yard punt. First we're backed up on *our one*, and just one play later they're backed up on *their one*. It's a pro record.

Even if you never kick a 98-yard punt, however, you can still be a good punter. Here are a few of the basic tips that good punters will give you (exchange the words *right* and *left* if you kick left-footed):

Good Rhythm: Don't try to kick the ball with all your might. Just try to have a good, steady rhythm to your kick. Ray Guy of the Los Angeles Raiders is probably the best punter of our time, and he says, "If I ever try to kick one really hard, I usually don't make good contact with the ball. So I just do what I call 'smoothing the ball.' I don't overstride. I don't swing all-out. I just try to have the same swing on every punt. A nice rhythm with a fluid motion."

Two Steps: Be a two-step punter. Don't take three steps to punt unless you absolutely have to. A three-step punter takes longer, and walks up closer to the rushers. It's easier for his punts to be blocked.

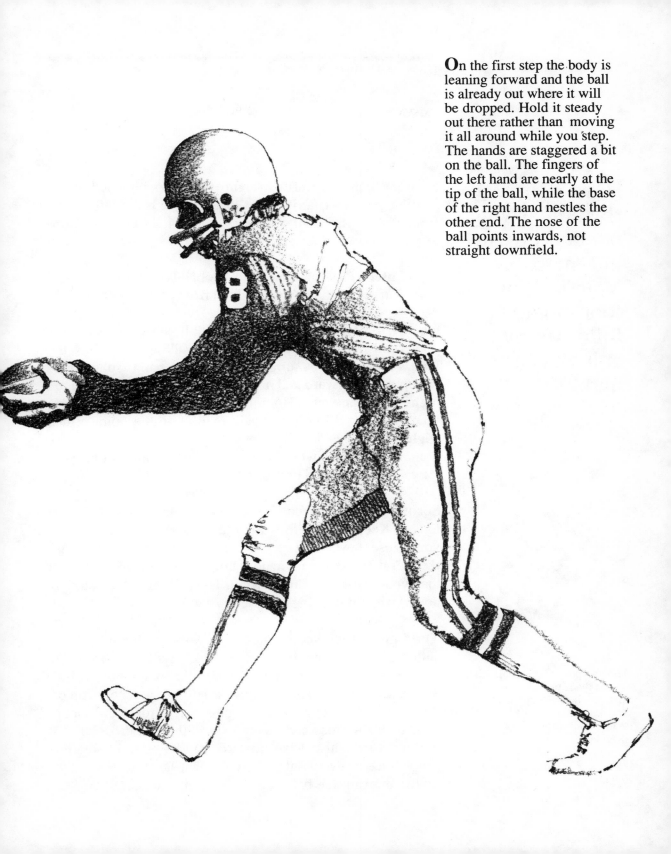

On the first step the body is leaning forward and the ball is already out where it will be dropped. Hold it steady out there rather than moving it all around while you step. The hands are staggered a bit on the ball. The fingers of the left hand are nearly at the tip of the ball, while the base of the right hand nestles the other end. The nose of the ball points inwards, not straight downfield.

Have a firm, rhythmic swing, but don't try to kill the ball. Your kicking foot should follow through at least head high.

The fat part of the ball hits out on the rounded part of the instep, where the shape of the ball and the shape of the foot match each other.

Stance: Stand up fairly straight, shoulders hunched over a bit. Put your feet fairly close together, with the left foot in front of the right about six inches or a foot. Extend your arms to give your center a target.

The Catch: Catch the ball in both hands. If the snap is off line, skip over and get your body in front of it. Don't reach.

The First Step: As you catch the ball, start forward with your right foot. Take a comfortable walking stride, not too long. As you do this, turn the ball in your hands so the laces are up. Lean forward and hold the ball out in front of you, no higher than the waist. Hold it out to the right just a bit, over your right leg. "I hold the ball level, with the point turned slightly to the inside," Guy says. "If you drop it with the nose pointed straight downfield, the back of the ball will hit your leg or ankle and spoil the punt."

Second Step: The second step, with the left leg, is just a bit longer. Keep leaning forward at the waist. If you lean back, you'll lose power. Take away the left hand first, then release the ball with your right hand. Drop it from a level no higher than your waist. The drop is vital. The ball should fall straight down, with no twisting or nose-diving.

The Punt: Drive your right leg up through the ball with a solid, whipping swing. Have a firm, rhythmic swing, but don't try to destroy the ball. Your right foot should follow through at least head high, and your left foot will come up off the ground. Swing your leg straight—don't cross it in front of your body. A cross-body swing slices the ball crookedly. If you want to punt the ball toward the left or right sideline, simply face that way right after the catch, step right toward the place you want the ball to go, and punt as usual.

You want to drop the ball from as low as you comfortably can. The less air time it has, the less it can wobble. Note the ball drops dead level, with the nose pointed slightly inward. Swing the leg solidly through the ball, with a smooth whip of the knee.

The kicker already has total concentration. His feet are close together, with his left foot slightly forward, and his eyes are zeroed in on the spot where the ball will be. He should keep his head down and his eyes burning into the ball until he kicks it. The holder marks the spot with one hand and reaches out to give the center a target with the other.

The Place Kick

The place kicker is a very important man on any football team. In the pros, the place kicker usually leads his team in scoring. And no man on the team is so frequently in position to win or lose a game in the last minute.

Place kickers are getting better all the time. Says Washington Redskin kicker Mark Mosely, "Ten years ago it was OK to make, say, 60% of your kicks. But in 1985 the pro average was 75%." Mosely himself holds the record for one season: 95% (20 out of 21).

Why are kickers getting better? They are working harder. They are kicking smarter. If you want to practice at it, and master the fine points, you can be a place kicker, too.

There are two completely different ways to kick place kicks: the newer soccer style and the older straight-ahead style. The soccer style is much more popular now (Mosely is the last straight-ahead kicker in the NFL). Here's why. First, a soccer-style kicker gets his whole instep on the ball, while a straight-ahead kicker just gets his toe into it. The soccer-style kicker has a much larger margin for error. If the straight-ahead kicker misses even just a bit, his kick will skid off to the side. Plus, if the holder doesn't get the ball down just right, the soccer-style kicker will have a better chance of getting good contact with the ball. Also, the soccer-style kicker gets more whip into his body and leg. And because the leg whips in a semi-circle, the leg moves through a larger range of motion than for a straight-ahead kicker. This means the leg of a soccer-style kicker is moving faster when it hits the ball. On the other hand, a straight-ahead kicker needs a lot of power. Usually straight-ahead kickers are fairly big. But even a little guy can use the soccer style, because of the leg-speed he gets.

To learn to kick soccer style, first learn to kick a soccer ball. That will get you used to the fluid, side-whipping motion. Says Raphael Septien, the Dallas Cowboys' excellent kicker, "One good drill is to take a soccer ball and just

Place kickers are getting better all the time. Says Washington Redskin kicker Mark Mosely, "Ten years ago it was OK for a pro to make, say, 60% of your kicks. But in 1985, the average was 75%."

247

> "You have to get that foot planted in exactly the right spot [on soccer-style kicks]," says Septien. "And as you plant, point those toes right toward the goal post."

kick it against a wall. Stand four or five feet from the wall, and just keep kicking and kicking. That will help groove your motion."

Here are some tips good soccer-style kickers give (again, exchange the words *right* and *left* if you are left-footed):

Stance: Put the tee down seven yards behind the center. (You can use a tee until you reach the pros. Most kickers prefer a two-inch tee). Take three comfortable steps straight back away from the tee, then two side-straddle steps to the left (so you are on the left of the tee as you face it). Put your feet a few inches apart, with your left leg slightly ahead. Lean forward at the waist.

First Step: As the ball hits the holder's hands, take a normal, comfortable step with your right foot. Get rolling right away, but don't overstride.

Second Step: This is one key to the kick. Take a fairly long stride, to build up momentum. Now, *plant that foot precisely*. Plant it about six or eight inches to the left of the ball, and right even with the ball (if you are using a two-inch tee). "You have to get that foot planted in exactly the right spot," says Septien. "And as you plant, point those toes right toward the goal post." Continue to lean forward. If you lean back, you will lose your power—and you'll kick the ball low.

The Kick: As your right foot draws back to kick, point the toes hard. Keep them pointed straight out throughout the kick. Whip your leg through the ball, and hit the ball about one and a half inches below center. Have what kickers call a "fast knee" so that your lower leg has a good whip in it. But don't over-kick. Like punters, place kickers try to have a comfortable, fluid motion. Follow through nice and high, and as

The soccer-style kick allows a full range of leg motion. It also affords a lot of whipping body action (see picture below). Note that the toes of the left foot (the plant foot) point downfield toward the goal post, and the toes of the kicking foot are kept pointed straight out like a ballet dancer's.

"You have to get your toe up and your ankle as rigid as possible [on straight-ahead kicks]," says Moseley. "You don't want the force of the ball to bend your foot down even a fraction. That would lose your power."

straight toward the goal posts as you can. "The less you turn," says Septien, "the more accurate you will be."

SOCCER-STYLE CHECKLIST: If you are kicking too far up in the air, your left foot (plant foot) is too far forward. If you are kicking too low, your foot is too far back (or you are leaning back). If you hook your kicks left, your foot is too close to the ball. If you slice balls right, your foot is too far away from the ball. Adjust your stride and your plant until your kicks are going where you want them.

STRAIGHT-AHEAD KICKING:

Stance: Take three comfortable steps straight back from the tee. "Line up with your right foot on an exactly straight line through the tee to the goal posts," says Moseley. Your left foot should be a bit in front. Lean forward at the waist.

First Step: Step with your right foot, a normal comfortable stride that gets you moving and starts your rhythm.

Second Step: Again, this step is longer to build up speed. Plant your left foot four to six inches to the left of the ball and eight to ten inches behind.

The Kick: As your right foot comes back, lock the ankle with the toe *up* as far as possible. "You have to get your toe up and your ankle as rigid as possible," says Moseley. "As you hit the ball, you don't want the force of the ball to bend your foot down even a fraction. That would lose your power." Whip your leg straight through the ball. Have a "fast knee" but don't over-kick. Hit the ball about one and a half inches below the center. "Your leg really has to maintain a straight line," Moseley says. "You have to be straight as a pendulum." Follow through higher than your waist.

The straight-ahead kicker sets the toes on his kicking foot in just the opposite way from the soccer style. Instead of being pointed down, they are locked up, in a rigid right-angle position with respect to the leg. The straight-ahead kicker also wears special square-toed shoes.

The Kicker's Mind

Kickers have to work in tough situations. They require more than a strong leg. They require a tough mind. A mind that won't crack under pressure.

If you want to be a kicker, you should be ready to work on your mind as much as you do on your kicking technique. Lots of guys can kick pretty straight when they're fooling around out on the practice field. But when you go out there during a game, that's a whole different story. Maybe you're a punter and you have to kick it from deep in your own end zone. Or maybe you're a place kicker and the whole game has come down to the last five seconds—and you.

These are tough situations. They require more than a strong leg. They require a tough mind. A mind that won't crack under pressure.

Wayne Sevier is the special teams coach for the Washington Redskins. And when Wayne talks about kickers, he is quick to talk about the mental requirements. "What we are looking for is someone who is mentally tough," Sevier says. "We need people who are real competitors, who can kick under pressure, who can miss one or two and come right back."

And Mark Moseley, the Redskins' place kicker for many years, agrees. "The mental part is much more difficult than the physical part," Moseley says. "It's the pressure, dealing with the pressure, that is the big challenge."

Your opponents aren't going to help you. A lot of times, just before a field goal, they'll call time out on you. They want you to walk around and think about the pressure and get so tight you can't kick straight. Plus, they're going to talk to you every chance they get. "The talking gets worse every year," says Ray Guy, the Raider punter. "They'll walk by you before the game and say, 'We're coming today Ray. We're going to block one.' They'll get to your mind if you let them."

How do you handle the pressure? What techniques can you use to make yourself mentally strong? Raphael Septien has several suggestions, and one of them is to practice positive thinking before the game comes up. "You have to load your mind with positive thoughts," Septien says. "You tell yourself you're a good kicker. You tell yourself you kick well under pressure. You fill your mind with positive thinking— and you don't doubt."

Another technique Septien uses is visualization. This is a technique used by many athletes for many different skills. The idea is to imagine being successful. Then you play that mental picture over and over in your mind. "I visualize that ball going right through the center of the uprights," Septien says. "Not just through the goal posts, but right through the center. I'll do this on the sideline getting ready for a kick, and then the first thing when I go out on the field. First you see it happen in your mind. Then you just turn your body loose and let it perform."

Something else that nearly every kicker does is to concentrate on the techniques of kicking in the time just before the kick. "You have to wall out the pressure," Guy says. "You can't start thinking about the crowd, or about the guys on the other team. And the easiest way to wall all that out is to focus on the exact steps you have to do to get your job done."

"You pick out the important things," Septien says. "Even before I go out on the field, I start to concentrate on my techniques. I focus on getting my left foot planted in the right spot. I focus on keeping my head down and my eyes on the ball. I think about a good free-flowing swing and a good follow-through. It's a very technical job, kicking. So you have to focus and get the details right. We're human beings, not machines. But as kickers we want to perform like machines—the same way every time."

This is just like the mental checklists we have been talking about. In the time before your kick, instead of worrying and getting nervous, you think about exactly what you are going to do. Then as you kick do one last thing: keep your head down until your kicking leg has followed through.

Visualization is a technique used by many athletes for many different skills. The idea is to imagine being successful. Then you play that mental picture over and over in your mind.

The Invisible Heroes

Now here are two really important guys that most football fans never think about at all: the snapper and the holder.

Now here are two really important guys that most football fans never think about at all. One is the *snapper*, the center who snaps the ball back on punts and place kicks. The other is the *holder*, the man who sets up the ball on place kicks.

A good holder makes a difference. In 1985, Mark Mosley was making 80% of his kicks, with only three misses all year. Then, in the 11th game, Redskin quarterback Joe Theismann got hurt—and Theismann had been Moseley's holder for a decade. After missing only three kicks in 11 games, without his regular holder Moseley missed eight in the last five games.

The holder's job is tough because there should only be 1.2 or 1.3 seconds from the time the snap begins until the time the kick is made. In that brief time, the holder has to catch the ball, set it down precisely on the right spot, and spin it to get the laces out of the way. The holder has to have good, quick hands and steady nerves. Usually he is a quarterback or wide receiver, somebody used to handling the ball precisely.

The snapper's job is at least as tough. Here are a few tips for doing it right (also see the caption at right). First, grip the ball with your good hand just as you would to throw a pass—but slightly more toward the point of the ball. "The throwing motion through your legs is not as efficient as a normal pass," says Steve Ortmayer, special teams coach of the Los Angeles Raiders. "That's why you need to grip more toward the point, to get leverage on the ball." Second, your good hand does most of the snapping. "Your other hand is simply placed on the ball with minimal pressure," Ortmayer says. Third, be sure to snap the ball crisply, and keep it, if anything, low. The holder or kicker has a chance to pick up a snap that hits the ground, but they can't do anything about one over their head. "As you snap," Ortmayer says, "follow through with your hands no higher than your knees. That will help keep the ball down."

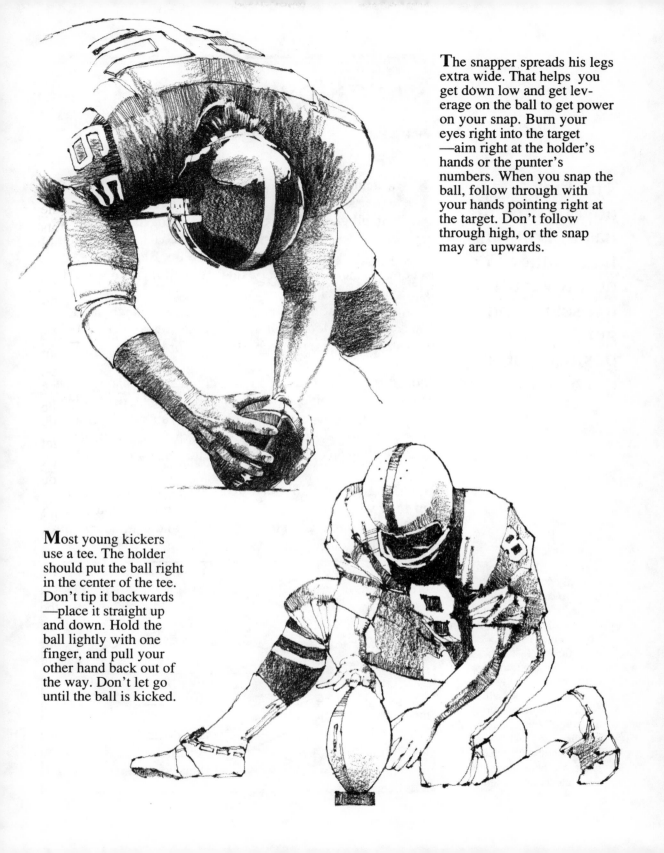

The snapper spreads his legs extra wide. That helps you get down low and get leverage on the ball to get power on your snap. Burn your eyes right into the target —aim right at the holder's hands or the punter's numbers. When you snap the ball, follow through with your hands pointing right at the target. Don't follow through high, or the snap may arc upwards.

Most young kickers use a tee. The holder should put the ball right in the center of the tee. Don't tip it backwards —place it straight up and down. Hold the ball lightly with one finger, and pull your other hand back out of the way. Don't let go until the ball is kicked.

Kick Coverage

The kick coverage team has to bottle up that runner. You don't want him to escape and get good field position, or a quick score.

Running down the field under a punt or kickoff to tackle the kick return man takes speed, courage and intelligence. "Kick coverage men have to go all-out," says Bob Matheson, the special teams coach for the Miami Dolphins. "But they also have to be aware. Blockers are going to come at them from every side. We tell them to keep their heads on a swivel."

An important new rule has made this a much safer job. Blockers can no longer hit the coverage men anywhere below the waist. There are two important tips for kick coverage men:

Lanes: Each kick coverage man should stay in his own *lane*. The people out wide should *stay* wide, and the people inside should remain evenly spaced as they run downfield. You never want to have two coverage men running one behind the other, leaving an open lane for the return man to find.

Breaking Down: You have to race all-out down the field, but then when you close in on the return man, you need to break down into a good hitting position and get under control to make the tackle. Don't overrun the man.

The punting team (black) can only send two men down to cover the kick immediately. At the snap of the ball, the two widest men (the *hot* men) streak downfield as fast as possible to confront the returner. Other men on the team must wait for the ball to be punted. They then sprint downfield, spread out evenly in *lanes*. The last two men, the punter and his *personal protector*, come down the field late as safetymen.

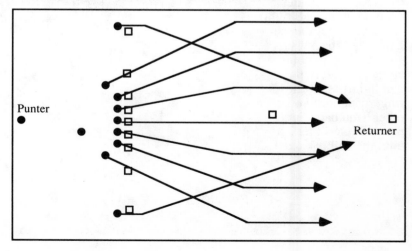

This sequence shows a kickoff return broken up by good kick coverage play. In this first picture, the return man has fielded the ball and started upfield. Up in front of him, his first group of blockers is forming into the *wedge*, getting shoulder-to-shoulder to blast a hole in the coverage.

Here the four-man wedge has formed up nicely, but two members of the coverage team have arrived. They are moving fast, and they have gotten down lower than the wedge men, so they have the better leverage position.

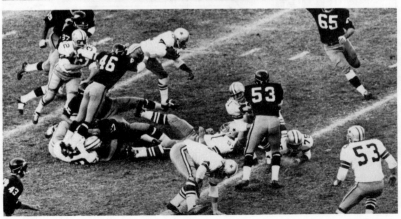

The wedge is completely leveled. In fact, those first two men have hit with such force into the wedge men that they have driven on through and upset the man with the ball. In the words of Miami coach Bob Matheson, "Coverage men can't go down there and stop in front of the wedge. If you start tippy-toeing, the wedge is going to pile-drive you. Attacking is the best defense you have."

257

Kick Returns

The kickoff and punt return men must be fast, have good eye-hand coordination and show plenty of courage.

The kickoff and punt return men must be fast, have good eye-hand coordination and show plenty of courage.

The kickoff returner has a fairly easy time catching the ball, but there is a trick you should know. "What you want is to judge the ball early and then catch it moving forward," says Miami's coach Bob Matheson. "That gets you to top speed a lot quicker." This is just like an outfielder who catches a fly ball while running forward in order to throw a man out at the plate.

The basic kickoff return is the *wedge* return (see pictures on previous page). The returner simply catches the ball and then follows his wedge at high speed. "It's basically a power play," says Larry Pasquale, the special teams coach of the New York Jets. "You pour it up in there and get what you can."

As compared with the kickoff return man, the punt return man is sometimes a more nimble athlete. He has to catch the punt and then immediately dodge people who are hurtling past him. For details on punt returns, see the illustrations below and on the opposite page.

This is the punt return known as *wall right*. Most of the blockers peel back down one sideline and form a wall. The returner tries to get over behind this wall and run down the sideline. The return team also puts two blockers (the *double vice*) on the "hot" men, the coverage men who can run down the field immediately. On the side away from the return, one of these men here sneaks in to rush the punter; at least one man must hurry the kick.

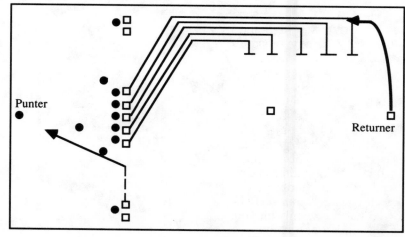

Punter

Returner

A punt gets very high and then it can knuckle or skid in the air in various ways. The only way to get comfortable is to catch a lot of punts in practice. As the ball is coming down, bend your legs so you can move quickly in any direction. Catch the ball out in front of you, in your hands. The ball comes nearly straight down, and if you catch it against your body it will almost certainly hit your pads and bounce away.

Glossary

audible After both teams have come up to the scrimmage line, a code called out by the quarterback, or by the defensive signal callers, to change a play that was called in the huddle.

automatic Same as *audible*.

backfield Players who line up behind the line of scrimmage. When used alone, backfield usually means "offensive backfield." See *defensive back*.

ball hawk A defensive player who is good at getting to passes to bat them down or intercept them.

bite To fall for a fake.

blitz When linebackers and/or defensive backs join the defensive linemen to cross the line of scrimmage at the start of the play and put pressure on the offense.

blocking Offensive players block for the man who has the ball by running into, or screening off, defensive players. Blockers may not grab with their hands nor trip with their feet. Up through high school, they also may not hit with their hands nor extend their arms out straight, though these moves are legal in college and the pros.

bomb Long pass.

breaking down The act of slowing down from a sprint to come under control and assume the basic hitting position.

bump-and-run A technique of pass defense: a defensive back lines up right in front of a receiver and tries to bump him off-stride before running with the receiver down the field.

burned When a defensive back is fooled by a pass receiver, especially if the pass is a long one.

center The middle man in the offensive line, responsible for snapping the ball to start every play. See page 42.

containment A defensive player turning a ball carrier back in toward the other defenders. See page 138.

cornerback, cornerman One of the two types of defensive backs; cornerbacks play wider, toward the sideline. See *safetyman* and see page 43.

cross block See page 112.

cut Sharp change of direction by a player.

dead spot An empty space in between defenders who are playing in a zone pass defense. Also called a seam.

defensive linemen Three to five men, ordinarily the front line of the defense; defensive tackles play to the inside, defensive ends to the outside.

deep Refers to the area downfield behind the defense where the offense might try to complete a long pass: as in "a deep pass," or, "he is playing deep."

deep zones In a zone pass defense, the zones farthest away from the line of scrimmage. As opposed to short zones.

defense The team that does not have possession of the ball.

defensive back, backfield Three or four players on the defense, two cornerbacks and one or two safetymen, usually lined up behind the defensive line and linebackers. Also called the secondary.

down See page 38.

downfield Toward the goal line defended by the defense.

down block An offensive lineman blocks the first defensive man who lines up to his inside. Also called blocking down.

draw, draw play A running play by the offense which starts out like a pass. The offensive linemen drop back as on a pass play and the quarterback also drops back, but then the quarterback hands the ball to a running back who has remained roughly where he originally lined up. This delayed run can work well if the defense is rushing in hard to stop the pass.

drop The retreat by a linebacker as part of playing pass defense, usually to a specific zone. Also occasionally used as an abbreviation for a quarterback's dropback.

dropback The retreat by a quarterback directly back from the line to give himself time and room to pass. See *roll out*.

end zone See page 36.

exchange point On any given play, the place in the offensive backfield where the quarterback hands the ball to the running back.

extra point (conversion) A score by the offense worth one point. See page 39.

fair catch A man in position to catch a punt may signal by raising his arm straight up in the air, and then catch the ball. If he does this, no one from the other team may tackle him, and he, in turn, may not return the punt. His team takes over on offense at the point where the ball is caught.

fake Any action by a player or players to fool one or more opposing players.

field position The place on the field where the offense has the ball. Good field position means you are closer to scoring while bad field position means you are bottled up back near your own goal. "We finally got field position" usually means "We finally got good field position."

first down See page 38.

field goal A kick by the offense worth three points. See page 39.

flat Area out to each side of an offensive formation, near the sidelines. Usually used only on a pass play, as, "A pass out in the flat."

free kick If a team receiving a punt signals for and makes a fair catch, it can then try a field goal, by place kick or dropkick, unimpeded by any defensive action.

fullback A running back. See page 42.

fumble A player who has legal control of the ball loses control of it, and the ball then drops to the ground or flies through the air.

guard, offensive guard One of the two offensive linemen who ordinarily line up on either side of the center. See page 42.

gang tackling Tackling the runner with as many people as possible.

gap The space between offensive blockers or defensive players.

gap defense When defensive linemen and linebackers are assigned to hold or charge through the gaps between blockers, rather than attack specific blockers.

goal posts (uprights) See page 36.

half A football game is divided into two halves, four one-quarter periods.

halfback See page 42.

handoff The quarterback or any player hands the ball to another player on his team.

hitting postion The basic posture, or position of the body, prior to making contact with an opponent. See page 58.

hook A pass route run by an individual pass receiver—straight down the field with a sudden stop to catch the ball, like a turn-in. Also, you *hook* a kick if you kick it so that it curves off to the side away from your kicking foot. See *slice*.

hot men The two men who line up the widest in a punt formation, the only men allowed to leave immediately when the ball is snapped. They are supposed to go as fast as they can.

interception A pass caught by the defense.

jab step Short step taken in one direction to push off in the other direction when leaving your stance. Used by most quarterbacks and wide receivers.

jam, the jam A defensive player uses his hands to hit an offensive player just under the shoulder pads and straighten him up.

juke A quick fake or move by one player to fool and get past an opposing player.

key, keys The particular player or players on the opposition whom you are assigned to watch at the start of a play—to tell you what play is coming and what to do.

kickoff At the start of each half, and after every score, one team kicks off to the other. You kick off from your own 40-yard line in high school and college, and from your own 35 in the pros. Your whole team must remain behind the ball until it is kicked. The ball is placed on a tee and kicked like a place kick.

lateral Throwing the ball laterally or backwards; this is legal at any time, at any point on the field, as often as desired, and any player on your team may catch it. See *pass*.

leverage A player who gets under his opponent and drives him upward with his shoulder or hands is said to have leverage.

line, linemen The players on offense and defense who line up on the line of scrimmage, usually with one or both hands on the ground. *Line* is also used as an abbreviation for *line of scrimmage*.

line of scrimmage An imaginary line through the forward tip of the football, from sideline to sideline, marking the forward progress of the offense before the start of a new play.

linebackers Defensive players who line up just behind (and sometimes right on) the line of scrimmage. See page 43.

long yardage situation When the offense needs to make a large amount of yardage for a first down or touchdown.

nose tackle The defensive lineman who lines up right in front of ("on the nose" of) the offensive center. Also called the *nose guard*.

offense The team that has possession of the ball.

offensive line Must consist of a minimum of seven players on the line of scrimmage; usually the center, two guards, two tackles and two ends.

on the nose Right in front of.

pass, forward pass Throwing the ball forwards. Legal only once per play; must be thrown from behind the line of scrimmage and caught only by an eligible receiver.

pass blocking Blocking by offensive linemen and backs to protect the passer.

pass defense The maneuvers by the defense to stop a passing play.

passing play See page 38.

pass rusher Defensive player charging in to get the passer.

pattern, pass pattern The coordinated movements, or routes, of all the pass receivers on any particular play.

pitchout When the quarterback tosses the ball sideways or backwards to a running back. Also called a *toss*.

place kick See page 39.

punt See page 39.

pursuit angle The angle a defender takes when running cross-field to cut off the ball carrier.

quarter Every football game is divided into four quarters—two halves with two quarters each.

quarterback The offensive leader and primary passer. Usually lines up right behind the center and takes the snap to start the play.

quick kick A type of punt, usually used on a down before fourth down, when the offense lines up as if for a regular play, but then has one of the backs punt the ball. Used to surprise the defense and, hopefully, secure better field position.

reading When a player watches the moves of one or more opposing players in order to determine which overall play or defense is being used.

receiver An offensive player used to catch (or receive) passes. Only five players are usually legal (or eligible) receivers: the two men who line up on the two ends of the offensive line, and three of the four men who line up in the backfield (the quarterback is not an eligible receiver if he takes the snap of the ball hand-to-hand from the center; if he takes it on a pass through the air, however, as in the shotgun formation, then he is eligible).

return man, returner The man designated to catch and run back a kick.

rip, rip move See page 214.

roll out The quarterback loops out toward the sideline to pass or run. See *dropback*.

route, pass route A pass receiver may run many different routes down the field to position himself to receive a pass. See page 188.

run support When defending against a running play, a defensive back running up toward the line of scrimmage to assume a pre-arranged responsibility.

runback Describes the return by a defensive man who has intercepted a pass or by a return man running with a kick after catching it.

running backs The men who line up behind the quarterback in the offensive backfield whose main job is running the ball.

running play See page 38.

rusher Short for pass rusher. Also used as a synonym for ball carrier.

rush men Pass rushers.

safety A two-point score by the defense. See page 39.

safety, safetyman One of the two types of defensive backs. Plays to the center of the field and often the farthest back from the line of scrimmage. See *cornerback*.

screen, screen pass A deceptive pass used against a defense that is rushing in hard to stop the usual passing game. The offensive line and quarterback drop back as on a normal pass, but then a running back (usually) and one or more blockers slip out to a side, or set up in the middle of the field, behind the line of scrimmage. The receiver catches the ball and his blockers form a screen of protection in front of him.

seam See *dead spot*.

secondary See *defensive backfield*.

shed A defensive player throwing a blocker out of his way.

shooting the gap A defensive player charging between two offensive linemen.

short yardage situation When the offense needs to make only only a small amount of yardage for a first down or touchdown.

short zones In a zone pass defense, the zones which are closer to the line of scrimmage. As opposed to deep zones.

sideline The out-of-bounds line up and down each side of the field. See page 36.

slice You slice a kick if you cause it to curve off to the same side as your kicking foot. See *hook*.

snap The pass of the ball, backwards and through his legs, by the center. The snap starts every play.

snap count The number, usually called out by the quarterback, on which the ball is snapped to start the play.

square-out A pass route run straight down the field, with a 90° break toward the sideline. See page 189.

spear To make a tackle or block head first, striking with the helmet. *Spearing is illegal and very dangerous. Do not spear.*

stance The position assumed by a player before the play begins to maximize his actions once the play has started.

sting See *jam*.

stripping the ball Pulling the ball loose from a runner to cause a fumble.

sweep A running play designed to circle wide around one flank of the defensive line or the other.

swim, swim technique See page 216.

tackle, offensive tackle Offensive linemen who ordinarily line up just outside the guards. See page 42.

tackling Bringing the man with the ball down to the ground—or decisively stopping his forward progress. Tacklers may hit and grab any way they want, except that they may not spear the runner (hit him with their helmets) and they may not grab his face mask.

tight end An offensive player who lines up on one end or the other of the offensive line, and in close (tight) to the other linemen. See page 42.

touchdown A score worth six points. See page 39.

trap, trap block When a defensive player is blocked (trapped) from the side. See page 110.

triple-option offense A type of running attack where key defensive men are not blocked and the quarterback decides whether to hand off, pitch out or keep the ball depending on what the unblocked defensive players do.

wedge The group of blockers who form a wedge-shaped wall in front of the return man on a kickoff.

wide receiver An offensive pass receiver who lines up wide, out toward the sideline, away from the offensive linemen. He may be one of the ends on the offensive line, or one of the backs.

wishbone A type of triple-option offense.

zone, zone defense A type of pass defense in which the defensive backs and linebackers are assigned to specific zones or areas of the field, rather than to specific offensive players. Zone can also mean the particular area covered by any particular defender.